PEACE

for

PARENTS

OF TEENS

A DEVOTIONAL

BETH SHRIVER

Charlotte, Tennessee 37036 USA

Library of Congress Control Number: 2010923175

ISBN-13: 978-0-9824832-5-1 (softcover)

Quotations from *Heroes of the Faith*, copyright © 1998, are used by permission of Barbour Publishing, Inc.

Scripture taken from the HOLY BIBLE, NEW INTERNATIONAL
VERSION®. Copyright © 1973, 1978, 1984 by International Bible Society.
Used by permission of Zondervan Publishing House. All rights reserved.

Scripture noted as NKJV is taken from The Holy Bible, New King James
Version. Copyright © 1982 by Thomas Nelson, Inc.

Scripture noted as NASB is taken from the NEW AMERICAN STANDARD
BIBLE®. Copyright © 1960, 1962, 1963, 1968, 1971, 1972, 1973, 1975, 1977,
1995 by The Lockman Foundation. Used by permission.

Scripture noted as WEB is taken from The World English Bible, copyright ©
2006.

Published in association with Hartline Literary Agency, Pittsburgh,
Pennsylvania 15235.

Cover design by Marisa Jackson.

10 11 12 13 14 15 16 17 18 19— 10 9 8 7 6 5 4 3 2 1

MANUFACTURED IN THE UNITED STATES OF AMERICA

DEDICATION

In dedication to my father, Robert Reier, who helped me write the questions for this project. Being a counselor for teens in the public school system for almost thirty years made him the most valuable asset in creating these devotionals. Through his encouragement I wrote these devotionals, originally for myself, but then he helped me to see the bigger picture of completing them to help others who were experiencing the same difficulties.

Also to the incredible women who helped me through a difficult time my teen went through: Kathy Whitthorne, Deb Finley, Laura Scott, Tammy Burrows, and Dee Plana, all great, godly women who were in my Bible study and/or served on leadership counsel with me. Thanks to Joan, my editor, for believing in this book, and my agent, Tamela, who didn't hesitate for a moment to represent me and this manuscript. And to my daughter for persevering. Without the help of each one of these individuals, this book would not have been published.

Note to Parents

Peace for Parents of Teens is for parents who experience struggles as their teenagers try to mature and discover their own identity in this world.

When my daughter was going through hardships, I wanted desperately to find encouragement to give me peace of mind before I laid my head down each night; something to help me feel that I wasn't a bad mother and that my daughter wasn't a bad child; comfort that let me know God was there in our midst and that He was seeing us through this storm. These devotionals provided just that—unconditional peace of mind.

Each week of this devotional has a topic. Each day of the week there is a verse of encouragement, a question, and a prayer that you can pour over your child. That nugget of peace will help get you through the night knowing you've called on God and covered your teen with hope. A tie-in paragraph addresses some of the struggles teens are dealing with today.

Peace for Parents of Teens can also be used as a parent-teen meditation if and when the teen is willing. Parents can choose whether to answer the questions themselves or to think about how their teen might answer. The questions are designed to personalize the verse and prayer, so use these tools to best fit your approach.

Before you turn the page, I want to tell you that no matter how you feel, you are a good parent. Any other kind wouldn't be reading this book.

In Him,
Beth

Week 1

FITTING IN

*Love the LORD with all your heart
and with all your soul and with all your strength.*
—DEUTERONOMY 6:5

What do you love more than God? How do you feel about others when you love God more?

With divorce breaking apart half of the marriages today, teens need to understand what it means to show love to others. As much as parents want to be good examples, it doesn't always happen. The more positive relationships our teens can experience, the more they will see the other half—the half that doesn't make the statistics.

•••••••••••

*I looked to Him, He looked on me,
And we were one forever.*
—CHARLES H. SPURGEON, FROM *THE SEARCH FOR GOD*

PRAYER: Lord, show ___ how to truly love,
to put aside self-consciousness and display affection,
to demonstrate care and value to the people
in (his/her) life. In Jesus' name, amen.

1

| DAY 2 | *For zeal for your house consumes me and the insults of those who insult you fall on me.* —PSALM 69:9 |

What are you most passionate about? Where does that kind of passion come from?

Passion can come from persons who have other beliefs and from those with seemingly no beliefs. You know what it's like to talk with someone whose belief system is different from yours. Even people close to us can take us off guard by expressing beliefs that conflict with ours. Teens need to be aware of all types of opinions related to faith and learn how to get through to people from the outside in.

• • • • • • • • • • •

*"I was at that time living like many atheists;
in a whirl of contradictions. I maintained that God did not exist.
I was also very angry with God for not existing.
I was equally angry with him for creating a world."*
—C. S. LEWIS, FROM *THE QUESTION OF GOD*

PRAYER: Lord, give ___ the courage to stand strongly for You, to use Your words as a sword that cuts through all things opposed to You. In Jesus' name, amen.

| DAY 3 | *Am I now trying to win the approval of men, or of God? Or am I trying to please men? If I were still trying to please men, I would not be a servant of Christ.* —GALATIANS 1:10 |

How do we know when we ought to seek the approval of others? How do we know when to stop?

Teens may try to fit in with many types of groups. Guide them to the right people. In our transient world, friends regularly come and go. Our teens need to be confident enough to wait for the right friends.

2

• • • • • • • • • • •

*"It is not the style of clothes one wears, neither the kind
of automobiles one drives, nor the amount of money one has
in the bank that counts. These mean nothing.
It is simple service that measures success."*
—GEORGE WASHINGTON CARVER,
FROM *GEORGE WASHINGTON CARVER: IN HIS OWN WORDS*

PRAYER: Lord, let ___ see You clearly
through the mass of worldly temptations. Guard
(him/her) from what appeals to the naked eye,
and lead (him/her) to what is good in Your eyes.
In Jesus' name, amen.

DAY
4

*Be devoted to one another in brotherly love.
Honor one another above yourselves.*
—ROMANS 12:10

**Do you think this verse applies to people who aren't believers
as well as to believers? Why?**

Teens face greater pressures today than ever before. They are
exposed to more carnality through the media and communications industry than we're aware of. As parents, we can only
fight against what we know is corruptive. It's crucial for us to not
only be aware of the choices our teens face so we can impose
limits, but also to teach our teens strong values so they will
make good choices when we're not there to guide them.

• • • • • • • • • • •

*"The relations of Christians to each other
are like the several flowers in a garden that have upon each
the dew of heaven, which, being shaken with the wind,
they let fall the dew at each other's roots,
whereby they are jointly nourished,
and become nourishers of one another."*
—JOHN BUNYAN, FROM *CHRISTIAN BEHAVIOR*

PRAYER: Lord, give ___ discernment when seeking friendship. Guide (him/her) to the people You know are beneficial, for only You know the true hearts of people and their motives. In Jesus' name, amen.

DAY 5

Set your minds on things above, not on earthly things.
—COLOSSIANS 3:2

How would your day change if you made a practice of thinking of heavenly things throughout?

Teens usually think for the moment. It is our job to help them look at the big picture. It may seem overwhelming to them at times, but the farther they see down the path that lies ahead, the better the decisions they will make.

• • • • • • • • • • •

"Lord, let me not live to be useless!"
—JOHN WESLEY, FROM SOUTHEY, *THE LIFE OF WESLEY*

PRAYER: Lord, teach ___ to live knowing (he/she) is with you this day. Help us to do and say what we should, feeling your presence when we choose our words and actions. In Jesus' name, amen.

DAY 6

"Because he loves me," says the LORD, "I will rescue him; I will protect him, for he acknowledges my name."
—PSALM 91:14

What do you think it would feel like to have the Lord reach down and rescue you when you are in trouble?

Without audibly hearing God's voice or feeling His bodily presence, we often forget to seek His wisdom, and instead make decisions on our own. But the Lord is with us, no matter what we need. We must constantly remind ourselves that our teens will never be alone.

• • • • • • • • • • •

"As sure as ever God puts His children into the furnace,
He will be in the furnace with them."

—CHARLES H. SPURGEON, FROM *HEROES OF THE FAITH*

PRAYER: Lord, remind ____ that You save (him/her) every day and for eternity and that not a day will pass in which (he/she) cannot turn to You. In Jesus' name, amen.

DAY 7

As the deer pants for streams of water,
so my soul pants for you, O God.
—PSALM 42:1

What do you most long for? Why?

What teens hope for will change as they mature. If we can instill in them a desire for what God wants for them, they will grow into godly adults. What a person yearns for and longs to be intertwines to help form character as he or she grows. It's never too early to begin guiding the desires of your teen.

• • • • • • • • • • •

"Don't take anyone else's word for God. Find Him
for yourself by inviting Jesus Christ to come into your life.
Then you, too, will know by the wonderful, warm tug
on your heartstrings that He is there for sure."

—BILLY GRAHAM, FROM *THE TUG OF GOD'S LOVE*

PRAYER: Lord, give ____ the discernment to set (his/her) heart on things that are worthy and good and to long for You above all others. In Jesus' name, amen.

Week 2

STRUGGLES

DAY 1

*Since you have kept my command to endure
patiently, I will also keep you from the hour of trial
that is going to come upon the whole world to test
those who live on the earth.*
—REVELATION 3:10

Is it hard for you to endure patiently? What makes it hard?

Teens often struggle to focus on long-term goals. God's never
ending promises remind us that the race is not for the here
and now, but for eternity.

• • • • • • • • • • •

*"He has plans, not problems for our lives. Before she died in the
concentration camp, my sister Betsie said to me, 'Corrie, your
whole life has been a training for the work you are doing here in
prison . . . and for the work you will do afterward.' "*
—CORRIE TEN BOOM, FROM *THE FIVE SILENT YEARS OF CORRIE TEN BOOM*
BY PAMELA ROSEWELL MOORE

PRAYER: Lord, give ___ the patience to persevere until
Your return, to feel your encouragement along the
way, and to know that (he/she) is on the right path.
In Jesus' name, amen.

DAY
2

Keep yourselves in God's love as you wait for the mercy of our LORD Jesus Christ to bring you to eternal life.
—JUDE 1:21

Do you love and forgive yourself as God does?

Whatever our teens have done, God forgives them when they come to Him. So should we. We are called as parents to mold and shape our children just as God does. Until they are molded to His will, we're not finished.

•••••••••••

"When we focus on God, the scene changes.
He's in control of our lives; nothing lies
outside the realm of His redemptive grace.
Even when we make mistakes,
fail in relationships, or deliberately make
bad choices, God redeems us."
—PENELOPE J. STOKES, FROM *FAITH HOPE AND FICTION*

PRAYER: Lord, let ___ feel Your compassion,
kindness, and understanding. Help me to show
(him/her) the kind of love only You can give.
In Jesus' name, amen.

DAY
3

And the God of all grace, who called you
to his eternal glory in Christ, after you have suffered
a little while, will himself restore you and
make you strong, firm and steadfast.
—PETER 5:10

What are some things you do or think about to help you get through suffering?

Struggles are unavoidable. We must follow our Father's example and let teens learn by persevering through hardships. He may not prevent your teen from going through the fire, but He will always deliver him or her.

• • • • • • • • • •

*"The happiness which brings enduring worth to life
is not the superficial happiness that is dependent
on circumstances. It is the happiness and contentment
that fills the soul even in the midst
of the most distressing circumstances."*
—BILLY GRAHAM, FROM *HEROES OF THE FAITH*

PRAYER: Lord, help ___ to seek the restoration
God has planned and avoid bitterness,
to know that whatever they go through,
it will work for the best in their lives as only
God knows. In Jesus' name, amen.

DAY 4

*Through faith we are shielded by God's power
until the coming of the salvation that is ready
to be revealed in the last time.*
—1 PETER 1:5

Do you feel that God shields you from difficult situations? Why or why not?

When teens get into difficult situations, God is there. If only they would learn to call on Him during those times, to truly know that He is with them, and to seek the comfort that can only be found in His love and care!

• • • • • • • • • •

*"Lord, I so often get myself into hot water.
I know the aroma of Your presence in my life
is evident at these times. People tell me so,
so I suppose it is true. But I don't like it one little bit.
But this I know, You 'always' keep hold
of the string! Thank you—You are the best.*
—JILL BRISCOE, FROM *GOD'S FRONT DOOR*

PRAYER: Lord, let ___ feel the strength of Your
protection, call on You in times of trouble,
and not feel alone when peers forsake (him/her).
In Jesus' name, amen.

DAY
5

*So that, having been justified by his grace, we might
become heirs having the hope of eternal life.*
—TITUS 3:7

**Do you really feel like you are justified and that God isn't
blaming you for your wrong actions?**

When teens feel despondent, where do they go? To a friend,
an addiction, or their heavenly Father? We must learn
about our teens' daily lives and seek to know their hearts. How
else can we guide them to where they need to be?

• • • • • • • • • • •

*"No matter what sin you have committed, no matter how dirty,
shameful or terrible it may be, God loves you."*
—BILLY GRAHAM, FROM *HEROES OF THE FAITH*

PRAYER: Lord, let ___ feel Your acceptance.
Encourage (him/her) to come back to You
when (he/she) strays. Remind (him/her) of Your
forgiveness in all things, no matter how ashamed
(he/she) may be. In Jesus' name, amen.

DAY
6

*I pray that out of his glorious riches he may strengthen
you with power through his spirit in your inner being.*
—EPHESIANS 3:16

**Can you put into words the different emotions you feel about
your relationships? Your relationship with Christ?**

Encourage your teen to be discerning. Famous, wealthy, and beautiful people are glorified in today's world, and often teens don't look deeper than the outward appearance. Learning how much they miss when they limit themselves to this way of thinking will help them to establish solid relationships.

• • • • • • • • • • •

"Am I ignitable? God deliver me from the dread asbestos of 'other things.' Saturate me with the oil of the Spirit that I may be aflame."
—JIM ELLIOT, FROM *HEROES OF THE FAITH*

> PRAYER: Lord, place Your holiness into ___'s heart and soul. Let (him/her) discern the difference between the outward appearance and the heart. In Jesus' name, amen.

 DAY 7

When I called, you answered me,
you made me bold and stouthearted.
—PSALM 138:3

When you pray to God, do you expect an answer? Why?

When teens are learning independence, it's hard for them to ask for help, especially if the answer isn't one they can hear or see. To lean solely on God is something we must not only try to teach our teens, but also strive to achieve ourselves. Our lives speak louder than our words.

• • • • • • • • • • •

"Let others say what they will of the efficacy of prayer, I believe in it, and I shall pray. Thank God! Yes, I shall always pray!"
—SOJOURNER TRUTH, FROM *THE NARRATIVE OF SOJOURNER TRUTH*

> PRAYER: Lord, help ___ to know you will answer according to Your will, not (his/hers). This is the difficult part of leaning on You, Lord. Help us learn to yield to Your will. In Jesus' name, amen.

Week 3
BELIEF

DAY 1

I know that my redeemer lives, and that in the end he will stand upon the earth.
—JOB 19:25

Do you have peace in believing that our Savior will return? Do you have doubts?

Even when teens feel shut out by the world, they need to know that they are always accepted by God. They are never unworthy in the heavenly Father's eyes, and they are loved by a God of second chances.

• • • • • • • • • • •

"When I was young I was sure of everything; in a few years, having been mistaken a thousand times, I was not half so sure of most things as I was before; at present, I am hardly sure of anything but what God has revealed to me."
—JOHN WESLEY, FROM *HEROES OF THE FAITH*

PRAYER: Lord, You have a place for ___ in Your kingdom. You have given (him/her) the promise of heaven and will not turn Your child away. Let (him/her) be comforted in knowing Your acceptance. In Jesus' name, amen.

13

Even though I walk through the valley of the shadow of death, I will fear no evil, for you are with me. Your rod and your staff, they comfort me.
—PSALM 23:4

What valley are you walking through? Are you alone?

Any addiction casts a dark shadow over one's life, but teens have God and you, as parents, to help them through. Maybe they're still struggling, but we are never to give up, any more than our Lord would give up on us.

• • • • • • • • • •

"Afflictions make the heart more deep, more experimental, more knowing and profound, and so, more able to hold, to contain, and beat more."
—JOHN BUNYAN, FROM *HEROES OF THE FAITH*

PRAYER: Lord, You are with ___ and will never leave (his/her) side. Nudge and stir (his/her) heart to know this at times when (he/she) feels shunned. In Jesus' name, amen.

Therefore, since we have been justified through faith, we have peace with God through our LORD Jesus Christ.
—ROMANS 5:1

How do you find peace? What keeps you from experiencing peace?

A teen can be led astray in the search for peace, not realizing true peace is found only in God. Doing what feels good can become a trap. Help your teen to know the high that God gives eternally and not turn to the temporary highs of the world.

• • • • • • • • • •

*"Character is the ability to carry out a good resolution
long after the excitement of the moment has passed."*
—CAVETT ROBERT, FROM *THINKEXIST QUOTES*

PRAYER: Lord, let ___ feel the calming
of your streams in (his/her) desert. No matter
how lost (he/she) is amid the vast hills of sand,
you are the oasis that can quench (his/her) thirst
as no other can. In Jesus' name, amen.

*We are hard pressed on every side, but not crushed;
perplexed, but not in despair.*
—2 CORINTHIANS 4:8

**When have you felt the most desperate? What do you feel
desperate about now?**

Depression has become more common but also more treatable in teens. Nonetheless, we hesitate to medicate and seek council, feeling that will show weakness or give reality to the problem. We need to seek wisdom to help our teens, and then do whatever God calls us to do.

• • • • • • • • • • •

*"The Lord gets his best soldiers out of the
highlands of affliction."*
—CHARLES H. SPURGEON, FROM *HEROES OF THE FAITH*

PRAYER: Lord, don't let ___ despair. Help (him/her)
to trust You. For we know God is the almighty
Healer, and we need nothing if we only trust
in His powers. In Jesus' name, amen.

DAY 5

So we fix our eyes not on what is seen, but on what is unseen. For what is seen is temporary, but what is unseen is eternal.
—2 Corinthians 4:18

How great is your need to have material things? How do you feel when you don't have the things you need or want?

The desire to have the latest fashion or the best grade is strong. Teens often don't feel that they fit in if they don't have the material things and status their friends do. Learning where the stopping point is in seeking these things will help them to make wise decisions.

•••••••••••

"We can stand affliction better than we can prosperity, for in prosperity we forget God."
—Dwight L. Moody, from *Heroes of the Faith*

Prayer: Lord, help ___ to see that now is temporary. Help (him/her) to work on building character and not to focus only on what shows on the outside. In Jesus' name, amen.

DAY 6

For we know, brothers loved by God, that he has chosen you.
—1 Thessalonians 1:4

Do you realize that God has chosen you? What's special about that?

Rampant bullying can challenge a teen's self-esteem. Knowing that Christ will always accept and protect them will provide support in dealing with those who act this way. Help your teen not only to stand up against this abuse when it is directed at them, but also to support and defend other victims of bullying.

••••••••••

*"Have you ever felt his presence through the kindness
of a stranger? Through the majesty of a sunset or the mystery
of romance? Through the question of a child or the commitment
of a spouse? Through a word well spoken or a touch well timed,
have you sensed Him?"*

—MAX LUCADO, FROM *THE GIFT FOR ALL PEOPLE*

PRAYER: Lord, let ____ know how special (he/she)
is to You, the creator of the universe. Help (him/her)
to feel worthy of being loved by the Almighty One
who created (him/her). In Jesus' name, amen.

*This is the confidence we have in approaching
God. That if we ask anything according
to his will, he hears us.*
—1 JOHN 5:14

**Do you believe that God hears your prayers? Why do you feel
that he does or doesn't?**

Teens don't always ask God for what they need for fear they
won't be heard. Scripture such as this one can help them
realize how precious God holds our prayers and that he hears us.

••••••••••

*"Lord, teach us to pray. Some of us are not skilled in the art of
prayer. As we draw near to you in thought, our spirits long for
your Spirit, and reach out for you, longing to feel you near."*

—PETER MARSHAL, FROM *CHAINS THAT BIND*

PRAYER: Lord, let ____ have the assurance that You are
listening. Teach (him/her) to be confident of your
love and come boldly before You with an open heart
in confession. In Jesus' name, amen.

Week 4

MATERIALISM

*For it is by grace you have been saved,
through faith—and this not from yourselves,
it is the gift of God.*
—EPHESIANS 2:8A

**What is the best earthly gift you have ever received? How
often do you think about and appreciate that gift?**

Our intentions are good in wanting only the best for our kids,
making it easy to overdo when we give gifts. To help keep
our lives in perspective, we need to take a step back and examine what the best gift for our teen really is.

• • • • • • • • • • •

*"In all our efforts to provide 'advantages'
we have actually produced the busiest, most competitive,
highly pressured, and over-organized generation
of youngsters in our history."*
—EDA J. LESHAN, FROM *MEDITATIONS FOR PARENTS WHO DO TOO MUCH*

PRAYER: Lord, open ____'s eyes to the importance
of the best gift (he/she) has ever received.
Turn (him/her) focus from the material world
and into Yours. In Jesus name, amen.

We all, like sheep, have gone astray, each of us has turned to his own way. And the LORD has laid on him the iniquity of us all.
—ISAIAH 53:6

Do you ever feel like running away? What is it that makes you feel that way?

Teens often look for the easy way out of problems they face and try to avoid the consequences of their actions. As they develop maturity and experience, we hope they will learn that they can't run from sin, but only find peace with themselves in the Lord.

• • • • • • • • • • •

"To be content with what we possess is the greatest and most secure of riches."
—CICERO, FROM *WISE WORDS AND QUOTES*

PRAYER: Lord, give ___ wisdom not to make rash decisions, to learn to see the result of (his/her) behavior, and to come to You for wisdom. In Jesus' name, amen.

Because on this day atonement will be made for you, to cleanse you. Then, before the LORD, you will be clean from all your sins.
—LEVITICUS 16:30

What would you have to do to feel totally clean?

The labels placed on our teens can be hard to change. Others may not forgive or be willing to let a person change. Help your teen to rest in the forgiveness of the Lord, the only way to truly become clean.

• • • • • • • • • • •

Few rich men own their own property. The property owns them.
—ROBERT INGERSOLL, FROM *FAMOUS WORDS AND QUOTES*

PRAYER: Lord, let ___ know that You see (him/her) as pure and clean. Help (him/her) drink that in and accept Your promise as truth. In Jesus' name, amen.

Greet one another with a kiss of love.
Peace to all of you who are in Christ.
—1 PETER 5:14

Who are your friends? What is it about them that makes you consider them your true friends?

A teen's friends can quickly turn into enemies and vice versa. Not knowing one day to the next who to count on leads to insecurity and loneliness. For teens to know that their Savior is always with them no matter what the day was like or what friends have said or done can bring more comfort than any human can ever give.

• • • • • • • • • •

"A true friend doesn't care what I've done
or where I've been; there's an unconditional
commitment that will never die."
—MICHAEL W. SMITH, FROM *365 DAY BRIGHTENERS TO WARM YOUR HOME*

PRAYER: Lord, help ___ to love (his/her) friends and (his/her) enemies, to live as Christ did in forgiving and not judging, and to accept others no matter what their transgressions may be. In Jesus' name, amen.

Grace, mercy and peace from God the Father
and from Jesus Christ, the Father's Son,
will be with us in truth and love.
—2 JOHN 1:3

Do you offer mercy to others? Think of times when you've done this. How did you feel afterward?

When teens are up, sometimes they forget those who are down. It's a constant struggle to stay on top and not get bumped and bruised along the way. Teens who choose to be an example of mercy help their peers learn how to treat one another with respect as Christ did.

• • • • • • • • • • •

"It is wonderful how much may be done
if we are always doing."
—THOMAS JEFFERSON, FROM *PATCHES OF GODLIGHT*

PRAYER: Lord, remind ___ not to leave anyone behind, to show kindness where needed, not just when it's expected. Help (him/her) to do the unexpected and accept those whom others do not. In Jesus' name, amen.

DAY
6

The grace of the LORD Jesus be with God's people.
—REVELATION 22:21

What are some words that describe kindness as you have experienced it?

Through helping people who are less fortunate, teens' eyes can be opened to the situations some of their peers face as well. Mission trips are one way to discover how others who are less fortunate live, but you don't have to cross an ocean to do good works. There are those in need in our own neighborhoods.

• • • • • • • • • • •

"We can love Jesus in the hungry, the naked,
and the destitute who are dying. . . . If you love,
you will be willing to serve. And you will find Jesus
in the distressing disguise of the poor."
—MOTHER TERESA, FROM *HEROES OF THE FAITH*

PRAYER: Lord, give ___ the opportunity to give charity to others. Create a stirring in (his/her) heart to want to help those in need and to recognize and act when that opportunity arises. In Jesus' name, amen.

DAY
7

He is the atoning sacrifice for our sins, and not only for ours but also for the sins of the whole world.
—1 JOHN 2:2

Jesus sacrificed himself for everyone. When you think of the people for whom you have sacrificed, how big is your world?

At times our sacrifices don't seem to be enough compared to the need, but God acknowledges our efforts. Whenever we feel we've given all we can, Christ gives us strength to do more.

• • • • • • • • • • •

"The greatest griefs are those we cause ourselves."
—SOPHOCLES, FROM *QUOTATIONS IN CULTURE AND HUMANITIES*

PRAYER: Lord, help ___ to love Jesus for what He has done for each one of us, to never forget or take for granted the depths and lengths to which Christ went to save us. In Jesus' name, amen.

Week 5
ANGELS

DAY
1

See, I am sending an angel ahead of you
to guard you along the way and to bring you
to the place I have prepared.
—EXODUS 23:20

Do you believe in angels? Why or why not?

Teens today need a guardian angel, and they need to be reminded of its presence. We often imagine that little devil on our shoulder, but we forget to place an angel on the other one.

• • • • • • • • • • •

"Philosophy will clip an angel's wings."
—JOHN KEATS, FROM *PATCHES OF GODLIGHT*

PRAYER: Lord, keep ___'s angel close and ready
to protect and do battle for (him/her). Keep
(him/her) on the straight and narrow and safe
from physical harm. In Jesus' name, amen.

In all their distress he too was distressed,
and the angel of his presence saved them.
In his love and mercy he redeemed them; he lifted
them up and carried them all the days of old.
—ISAIAH 63:9

Who do you look to in times of trouble? How has that helped in times past? Will you continue to go there?

A good mentor can be invaluable to teens. Another Christian adult who shares your moral standards and values can teach your teen things you cannot simply because it's not coming from you.

• • • • • • • • • • •

The golden moments in the stream of life rush past us
and we see nothing but sand; the angels come to visit us,
and we only know them when they are gone.
—GEORGE ELLIOT, FROM *MEDITATIONS FOR PARENTS WHO DO TOO MUCH*

PRAYER: Lord, place a person of Christian integrity into ___'s life. Make it Your choice, because You are the only one who can know whom ___ will listen to and go to when (he/she) can't come to me. In Jesus' name, amen.

But the angel said to them, "Do not be afraid.
I bring you good news of great joy that
will be for all the people."
—LUKE 2:10

What are you afraid of? Is it ever okay to be afraid? Why or why not?

You may have heard it said that our weaknesses might turn out to be our strengths. What we fear we can't do might be exactly what we are good at. Sometimes we need a little heavenly persuasion to get our teens to a place where they can find out.

• • • • • • • • • •

"The magnitude of life is overwhelming.
Angels are here to help us take it peace by peace."
—LEVENDE WATERS, FROM *MEDITATIONS FOR PARENTS WHO DO TOO MUCH*

PRAYER: Lord, teach ____ to have confidence in you
when (he/she) is afraid. Help (him/her) face fears
straight on and know you have the outcome under
control. In Jesus' name, amen.

DAY 4	*An angel from heaven appeared to him* *and strengthened him.* —LUKE 22:43

**Where do you find your strength? Do you find strength in
more than one place? Which is the most dependable?**

Having something God-based at the core of teens' social lives is crucial, whether it is church or youth group, Christian friends or family. They need that touchstone to which they can always return.

• • • • • • • • • •

"The soul at its highest is found like God,
but an angel gives a closer idea of Him.
That is all an angel is, an idea of God.
—MEISTER ECKHART, FROM *WISE WORDS AND QUOTES*

PRAYER: Lord, help ____ to lean on You and
not on things of this world for strength. Keep
(him/her) from the quick fixes that don't last.
Help (him/her) to learn that You are the answer
they seek. In Jesus' name, amen.

*Last night an angel of the God whose I am
and whom I serve stood beside me.*
—ACTS 27:23

Do you ever let yourself feel the power of angels?

Teens don't need to understand everything, just to believe. Do they feel that they have that kind of faith? If not, what's holding them back? Getting past those barriers will set them free.

• • • • • • • • • • •

*"I saw the angel in the marble and carved
until I set him free."*
—MICHELANGELO, FROM *PATCHES OF GODLIGHT*

PRAYER: Lord, let ___ feel the strength of (his/her) guardian angel and know that angels are with (him/her) through good and bad to protect and guide. In Jesus' name, amen.

*Are not all angels ministering spirits sent
to serve those who will inherit salvation?*
—HEBREWS 1:14

Do you know how huge it is that you have angels ministering to you?

Remind your teens that they are never alone. That they have angels watching over them can be hard for them to wrap their heads around, but once you get them there, the comfort they experience will be never ending.

• • • • • • • • • • •

*"Silently, one by one, in the infinite meadows
of heaven, blossomed the lovely stars,
the forget-me-nots of the angels."*
—HENRY WADSWORTH LONGFELLOW, FROM *QUOTATIONS BOOK*

PRAYER: Lord, let ___ know the power of Your angels
here to serve (him/her). Help (him/her) to take
comfort in the knowledge that Your heavenly angels
surround (him/her) in all the trials of life.
In Jesus' name, amen.

DAY 7

*Do not forget to entertain strangers, for by so
doing some people have entertained angels
without knowing it.*
—HEBREWS 13:2

**Have you ever felt as if you were in the presence of an angel?
When? If not, what do you think it would feel like?**

How it would comfort teens to recognize God's power on
earth! We often don't know whether something that happened was just a coincidence or directed by God. We learn to
discern this as we grow closer to God. Helping teens to learn
how to make this distinction will enable them to see the angels
in their world.

• • • • • • • • • •

*"Angels deliver fate to our doorstep,
and anywhere else it is needed."*
—JESSI LANE ADAMS, FROM QUOTES GARDEN

PRAYER: Lord, pour out the calming awareness
of Your angels on ___. Make known to (him/her)
the power You have here on earth to shield
and protect (him/her) from harm.
In Jesus' name, amen.

Week 6

ENDURANCE

> "The LORD bless you and keep you; the LORD make his face shine upon you and be gracious to you; the LORD turn his face toward you and give you peace."
> —NUMBERS 6:24-26

Are you aware of the Lord's blessings? What difference does it make in your daily life when you feel His blessing? When you don't?

Staying connected with God even in the midst of doubt will bring comfort to teens. They might not always know it, but He is always there for us if we only go to Him and take pleasure in His guidance and love.

• • • • • • • • • • •

"Cultivate my heart, Lord, so I may catch every word that falls from heaven, every syllable of encouragement, every sentence of rebuke, every paragraph of instruction, every page of warning. Help me to catch these words as the soft, fertile soil catches seeds."
—KEN GIRE, FROM *365 DAY BRIGHTENERS TO WARM YOUR HOME*

PRAYER: Lord, may ___ feel Your graciousness. Let Your spirit be recognized and cherished and help us to do Your will. Help us to recognize that You want great things for us and to prosper. In Jesus' name, amen.

| DAY 2 | *May the God who gives endurance and encouragement give you a spirit of unity among yourselves as you follow Christ Jesus.*
—ROMANS 15:5 |

Where do you get endurance? What do you think it feels like to receive endurance and encouragement from God?

For teens, who live only for the moment, developing endurance may seem overwhelming. Sometimes just getting through the day or a certain situation can be exhausting and distract him or her from what's really important. Putting God as the center—always—will help them to see things through to the end.

• • • • • • • • • • •

"Prayer does not fit us for the greater work; prayer is the greater work."
—OSWALD CHAMBERS, FROM *PATCHES OF GODLIGHT*

PRAYER: Lord, teach ___ how to pace (himself/herself) to finish well. Remind (him/her) that You will provide the strength needed to get through the struggles (he/she) is dealing with and that (he/she) is never alone in facing what is ahead. In Jesus' name, amen.

| DAY 3 | *The God of peace will soon crush Satan under your feet. The grace of our LORD Jesus be with you.*
—ROMANS 16:20 |

What does the promise in this verse mean to you in your daily life?

It's hard for teens to stay on the narrow path. Satan does his best to defeat them at any cost. That God can crush both the Enemy and the sin in our lives is something to boast about and find courage in. The grace of Christ makes all things new.

• • • • • • • • • •

"He prayed me into a good frame of mind,
and if he had stopped there, it would have been very well;
but he prayed me out of it again by keeping on."
—GEORGE WHITEFIELD, FROM *PATCHES OF GODLIGHT*

PRAYER: Lord, help ___ to recognize the Evil One's
trickery and resist it. Keep Satan's manipulations
at bay and don't let ___ be blinded by the world's
allure. In Jesus' name, amen.

DAY
4

May the grace of the LORD Jesus Christ,
and the love of God, and the fellowship
of the Holy Spirit be with you all.
—2 CORINTHIANS 13:14

Do you call on the Father, Jesus, and the Holy Spirit when you have a need? How has God answered you in the past?

Many obstacles keep teens from enduring. After trying to figure things out on their own and asking friends and others for advice, they might finally become desperate enough to turn to the Lord. We pray that instead of waiting, they learn to seek Him first in times of trial.

• • • • • • • • • •

"There is nothing that makes us love someone
so much as praying for him or her."
—WILLIAM LAW, FROM *PATCHES OF GODLIGHT*

PRAYER: Father, Jesus, and Holy Spirit help ___ see that
(he/she) has the holy Trinity on (his/her) side to fight
the evil of the world. Remind ___ that the Evil One's
captivity is never friendly. Things of this world that
might satisfy for a little while will never compare to
your everlasting love and care. In Jesus' name, amen.

33

DAY
5

May the God of peace . . . equip you with everything
good for doing his will, and may he do work in us
what is pleasing to him, through Jesus Christ,
to whom be glory for ever and ever. Amen.
—HEBREWS 13:20-21

Do you feel God working in you? Think of times when you have felt it.

Knowing that God is the key that unlocks the door for him or her to do good works will help your teen to endure. Human works apart from God are ultimately meaningless. Only He can show us how to direct our path so our works have eternal value.

• • • • • • • • • • •

"Surprise me, Lord, as a seed surprises itself."
—GEORGE HERBERT, FROM *PATCHES OF GODLIGHT*

PRAYER: Lord, let ___ see the good works
You are doing in and through (him/her).
Help (him/her) to be an example, Lord, to know
that You are working great things in (his/her) soul
and life. Remind ___ that You equip us to do
whatever You ask and that (he/she) has power
to succeed in Your name. In Jesus' name, amen.

DAY
6

. . . who have been chosen according to the foreknowl-
edge of God the Father, through the sanctifying work of
the Spirit, for obedience to Jesus Christ and sprinkling
by his blood: Grace and peace be yours in abundance.
—1 PETER 1:2

Do you feel that you have been chosen by God? How does that help you to endure?

Knowing that they have been chosen by God can strengthen teens to endure. When they have given in to peer pressure to do something wrong, they won't feel worthy of blessing or be able to move on until they know that the past is forgiven and their relationship with us and with God is restored.

• • • • • • • • • •

"Lord, make me see thy glory in every place."
—MICHELANGELO, FROM *PATCHES OF GODLIGHT*

PRAYER: Lord, even if ___ has lost (his/her) purity, help (him/her) to feel wholesome again. Satan makes ___ feel impure in so many different ways. Let (him/her) feel Your hand wash (him/her) as white as snow. In Jesus' name, amen.

| DAY 7 | *Blessed are all who take refuge in him.*
—PSALM 2:12B |

Can you think of a time you needed protection? Did you choose to take refuge in God? Why or why not?

If teens can learn to see through the "stuff" of our culture and put God first, they will find the inner peace that will help them to endure. It's hard to have clear vision when media, games, music, and literature increasingly blur truth. We need to help our teens learn where to draw the line on the influences they allow into their lives and take refuge in God.

• • • • • • • • • •

"O Lord, that lends me life, lend me a heart
replete with thankfulness."
—SHAKESPEARE, FROM *PATCHES OF GODLIGHT*

PRAYER: Lord, let ___ see that (his/her) body is a temple made by You. Help (him/her) to keep (his/her) body and mind clean from the ungodly influences of our culture so (he/she) can always come to You with thanksgiving. In Jesus' name, amen.

Week 7

FELLOWSHIP

DAY
1

. . . with whom I once enjoyed sweet fellowship as we walked with the throng at the house of God.
—Psalm 55:14

At what times do you find it easiest to enjoy God's fellowship?

We can help our teens feel whole again by placing no judgment on them, no matter what they've done. Finding peers who have been through some of the same trials might help them to see the forgiveness they need to know that God has already given.

• • • • • • • • • •

"It is in the shelter of each other that people live."
—Irish Proverb, from *Patches of Godlight*

> PRAYER: Lord, help ___ to find a friend
> whom (he/she) can trust. Let it be someone from
> Your flock with whom ___ can be mutually
> accountable. Let it not only be a fellowship
> of past times but also of You and within
> Your will for (him/her) in (his/her) walk
> with You. In Jesus' name, amen.

For everything that was written in the past was written to teach us, so that through endurance and the encouragement of the Scriptures we might have hope.
—ROMANS 15:4

God has already chosen to walk with us. We have to make the choice to walk with Him also. Have you deliberately done this?

The decision to walk with Christ is a big commitment that a teen can only make for himself or herself. Talking with your teen on a regular basis about this decision and what led him or her to believe in Christ will help to reinforce that commitment. Writing down his or her testimony is also a good way to really think it through.

• • • • • • • • • •

"In the name of Jesus Christ, who was never in a hurry, we pray, O God, that You will slow us down, for we know that of eternity before us, make us take time to live, time to get reacquainted with You, time to enjoy Your blessings, and time to know each other."
—PETER MARSHALL, FROM *DAILY CHRISTIAN QUOTE*

> PRAYER: Lord, give ___ the strength to say no when Satan calls and continue to walk with You. Keep (his/her) walk steady, on the straight and narrow. Let (him/her) go to You in times of trouble and not seek the temporary comforts of the world. In Jesus' name, amen.

Then those who feared the LORD talked with each other and the LORD listened and heard. A scroll of remembrance was written in his presence concerning those who feared the LORD and honored his name.
—MALACHI 3:16

How does it help you when you talk with other believers about things you are concerned about?

Teens don't always know when a person is "real" in his or her convictions. They need to be aware of how seductive Satan is so he won't tempt them in obvious ways. By teaching discernment, you will help your teen discover what is of God and what is not.

•••••••••••

"Write to me often. Write freely, as I do to you.
Say many kind things, and say them without reserve.
They will be food for my soul."
—THOMAS JEFFERSON TO MARIA COSWAY,
FROM *365 DAY BRIGHTENERS TO WARM YOUR HOME*

PRAYER: Lord, let ___ feel the "good" fear when temptation arises. Let Your Holy Spirit stand guard to warn (him/her). Let the Spirit also protect (him/her) when (he/she) strays. In Jesus' name, amen.

DAY 4

Jesus called them together and said, "You know that the rulers of the Gentiles lord it over them, and their high officials exercise authority over them. Not so with you. Instead, whoever wants to become great among you must be your servant, and whoever wants to be first must be your slave—just as the Son of Man did not come to be served, but to serve, and to give his life as a ransom for many."
—MATTHEW 20:25-28

Is what Jesus says about being a servant the way we usually think? Why or why not?

Doing what is right is not always sociably acceptable for teens. They may feel that trying to be a servant to others will make them vulnerable to being taken advantage of. Having godly friends who stand by them will help them have courage. And as they mature, they will learn that the real power lies in servanthood.

•••••••••••

*"There are no words to express the abyss between
isolation and having one ally. It may be conceded
to the mathematician that four is twice two. But two is not
twice one; two is two thousand times in one."*
—G.K. CHESTERTON, FROM *PATCHES OF GODLIGHT*

PRAYER: Lord, help ___ to develop an attitude
of servanthood. Let friends with the same morals and
values surround (him/her). Help (him/her) focus on
You when others try to take advantage.
In Jesus' name, amen.

DAY
5

*"A new command I give you: Love one another.
As I have loved you, so you must love one another."*
—JOHN 13:34

**Are we able to truly love one another when we harbor feelings
of jealousy, anger, envy, and ill will? Who would you find it
most difficult to love as Jesus loves you?**

Loving others as Christ loved them can be a real struggle for
teens. Being cool is first and foremost for most teens, and
that may mean treating those who aren't considered cool in
ways that aren't loving. Remind your teen often of how much
God loves them and encourage him or her to extend that love to
even those society may not see as worthy.

• • • • • • • • • • •

*"He who does not live in some degree for others
hardly lives for himself."*
—MONTAIGNE, FROM *PATCHES OF GODLIGHT*

PRAYER: Lord, keep ___ from the attitude of the
world that there are those who aren't worthy of love.
Help (him/her) to be a friend to others and to love as
You love. In Jesus' name, amen.

DAY 6

If you have any encouragement from being united with Christ, if any comfort from his love, if any fellowship with the Spirit, if any tenderness and compassion, then make my joy complete by being like-minded, having the same love, being one in spirit and purpose.
—PHILIPPIANS 2:12

Do you have the kind of tenderness and compassion toward others described in this verse?

Just as a cord of three strands is not easily broken, so also a group of peers who are of the same mind is very powerful. As teens join together in faith, they will strengthen one another to stand against temptation and to love others as Christ loves them.

• • • • • • • • • • •

"If you want to know your true opinion of someone, watch the effect produced in you by the first sight of a letter from him."
—SCHOPENHAUER, FROM *THINKEXIST QUOTATIONS*

PRAYER: Lord, bless ___'s friends and keep them together in Your name. Teach them to depend on one another for earthly support and refuge from the evils of the world as they depend on You for spiritual guidance and encouragement. In Jesus' name, amen.

DAY 7

Carry each other's burdens, and in this way you will fulfill the law of Christ.
—GALATIANS 6:2

Whose burdens are you carrying right now? Who is carrying yours?

Joining together to live out a Christ-like life provides incredible power. Teens don't always want to be a part of the family. This is the natural course of things as they work out their independence. But if you don't give up on family time, they will not wander too far from the nest until they are ready to fly.

• • • • • • • • • • •

*"The main thing about Christianity is not the work we do,
but the relationship we maintain and the atmosphere produced
by that relationship. That is all God asks us to look after,
and it is the one thing that is being continually assailed."*
—OSWALD CHAMBERS, FROM PATCHES OF GODLIGHT

PRAYER: Lord, let me know when ___ needs more
than I can give. Help us see through Your eyes what
is healthy independence and what is not and to keep
some special time for family. In Jesus' name, amen.

Week 8
FORTITUDE

Do not conform any longer to the pattern of this world, but be transformed by the renewing of your mind. Then you will be able to test and approve what God's will is—his good, pleasing, and perfect will.
—ROMANS 12:2

Is it possible to stop conforming to the pattern of this world? Can anyone do this completely?

Teens feel more pressure than we know, and it's easy for them to be pressed into the world's pattern. When the lines have been crossed, it's hard to go back. For our teens to learn to stand strong is a matter of survival. Keeping their eyes on God's goals for their lives will help them to do this.

• • • • • • • • • •

"It is strange that we prepare for everything except meeting God."
—BILLY GRAHAM, FROM *HEROES OF THE FAITH*

PRAYER: Lord, help ____ to renew (his/her) mind
to Your good, to search out what is right and not be
attracted to what is wrong, to feel good enough about
(himself/herself) to not go down the wrong path, all
for Your glory. In Jesus' name, amen.

Be joyful in hope, patient in affliction,
faithful in prayer.
—ROMANS 12:12

What situations in your life right now would be helped if you did what this verse says?

What we see as obstacles for our teens might not be what they are really struggling with. What we might see as apathy might just be a teen enduring his or her present situation. Guiding our teens to develop goals worthy of striving for that are in line with their abilities will help them to overcome obstacles that hinder them.

• • • • • • • • • •

"I have held many things in my hands, and I have lost them all;
but whatever I have placed in God's hands, that I still possess."
—MARTIN LUTHER, FROM *HEROES OF THE FAITH*

PRAYER: Lord, give ___ goals to keep (him/her)
focused on who (he/she) hopes to be. Let (him/her)
know (his/her) capabilities and go to You when
(he/she) is unable to handle a situation.
In Jesus' name, amen.

Be on your guard; stand firm in the faith;
be men of courage; be strong.
—1 CORINTHIANS 16:13

Can you do what this verse commands on your own? With the help of friends? With the help of God?

Throughout their lives, as teens achieve goals they will need to set new ones, and that can be unsettling. The pressures of the world make it easy to lose sight of the goals God has for us. Teens need to be on guard and stay strong so they keep moving forward on the right road.

• • • • • • • • • • •

*"A good mind, a good heart, warm feelings,
these are the most important things."*
—DALAI LAMA, FROM *MEDITATIONS FOR PARENTS WHO DO TOO MUCH*

PRAYER: Lord, help me look past ____'s anxiety
to the real problem. Let (his/her) outward actions
and words come from what is truly on (his/her)
heart. Show me the real struggles and needs (he/she)
has, and not only what ____ wants me to see.
In Jesus' name, amen.

DAY
4

*For he says, "In the time of my favor I heard you,
and in the day of salvation I helped you."*
—2 CORINTHIANS 6:2

**How does this verse relate to John 13:34, "A new command I
give you: Love one another. As I have loved you, so you must
love one another"?**

Teens don't always show their need to communicate. Uncertainty about where the boundaries are between information
that will get them in trouble and information they can share
without punishment can keep them from communicating.
Establishing an understanding beforehand as to what they can
tell you without getting into trouble might help them to open up.

• • • • • • • • • • •

"We knew the precise moment when to say nothing."
—OSCAR WILDE, FROM *PATCHES OF GODLIGHT*

PRAYER: Lord, let ____ feel a great need to communicate with You and seek your intervention. And by
doing so, let (him/her) feel safe in telling us what
(his/her) needs are. In Jesus' name, amen.

DAY 5

As a prisoner of the LORD, then, I urge you to live a life worthy of the calling you have received.
—EPHESIANS 4:1

How is it a good thing to be a "prisoner" of the Lord?

Teens who are just learning how to communicate their convictions can be misunderstood. Others may judge them and challenge them until they say things they don't mean. Role playing or showing them by example might help them to feel more comfortable in sharing their faith with their peers.

• • • • • • • • • •

"God, give us grace to accept with serenity the things that cannot be changed, courage to change the things which should be changed, and the wisdom to distinguish one from the other."
—REINHOLD NEIBUHR, FROM *PATCHES OF GODLIGHT*

PRAYER: Lord, remind ___ what is truly important in life, that sharing Your word and the salvation You offer is first and foremost in a person's life. Help (him/her) to live this out in (his/her) words and deeds. In Jesus' name, amen.

DAY 6

Fight the good fight of the faith. Take hold of the eternal life to which you were called when you made your good confession in the presence of many witnesses.
—1 TIMOTHY 6:12

Do you ever have to fight for your faith?

Drugs are one of the many temptations teens may be persuaded to take part in. Encourage them to stay strong. When they confess a difficult situation they were in and made the right decision, reward them by trusting them with more freedom.

• • • • • • • • • •

"The secret of success is constancy of purpose."
—BENJAMIN DISRAELI, FROM *PATCHES OF GODLIGHT*

PRAYER: Lord, help ___ to be clear about what the faith fight is and what we are called to do. Help (him/her) to maintain spiritual strength so that when called upon (he/she) is ready and able to battle for You. In Jesus' name, amen.

DAY
7

Let us fix our eyes on Jesus, the author and perfecter of our faith, who for the joy set before him endured the cross, scorning its shame, and sat down at the right hand of the throne of God.
—HEBREWS 12:2

How does it make you feel to look at Jesus in the way this verse describes Him?

There are many deceptive things in this world that appear as though they will stay the course, but will only let teens down. Understanding this takes trial and error, and hopefully experience will bring them back to their heavenly Father. Having clear goals and keeping their eyes on Jesus will help them to steer a straight course through life.

• • • • • • • • • • •

"Suffering is no argument of God's displeasure but a part of the fiber of our lives."
—FANNY CROSBY, FROM *HEROES OF THE FAITH*

PRAYER: Lord, help ___ to see the goals set before (him/her) as You have placed them in (his/her) life. Let (him/her) have the wisdom and ability to persevere and live up to all You have enabled (him/her) to do, all for Your glory. In Jesus' name, amen.

DAY
1

Your word I have treasured in my heart.
—PSALMS 119:11 (NASB)

Have you memorized Bible verses that you treasure? What are they?

The sword of God's Word can help teens to fight many battles. Encouraging them to think of a verse during times of hardship will help get them into the habit of thinking God's way instead of leaning on their own understanding.

• • • • • • • • • • •

"The Gospel is not only what the four evangelists have written, but the Word concerning the Son of God. It is the same Gospel no matter how many books have been written."
—MARTIN LUTHER, FROM *HEROES OF THE FAITH*

PRAYER: Lord, let ___ learn to live by Your holy Word, to be an example to others during good times and bad, to learn to thank You, seek guidance from You, and use Your strength and knowledge in every situation they encounter. In Jesus' name, amen.

DAY 2

Let the word of Christ dwell in you richly.
—COLOSSIANS 3:16

Has a Bible verse ever come to your mind at a time you especially needed it? When?

The Word of God is a certainty teens can believe in during good times and bad. When your teen seeks or needs advice during a rough time, guide him or her with the Word. Teaching your teen to celebrate with the Lord during prosperity and times of achievement will help him or her to believe that God wants us to be happy.

• • • • • • • • • •

*"Sin will keep you from this book (the Bible).
This book will keep you from sin."*
—DWIGHT L. MOODY, FROM *HEROES OF THE FAITH*

PRAYER: Lord, help ____ to desire the truth that will strengthen (him/her) to become the person you want ____ to be, to know Your Word and retain the wisdom gained from it. In Jesus' name, amen.

DAY 3

*When your words came, I ate them;
they were my joy and my heart's delight, for I bear
your name, O LORD God Almighty.*
—JEREMIAH 15:16

What do you usually look for to sustain you in difficult times?

Teens who learn the difference between true joy and the self-fulfillment the world tells them is their right have much to lean on. In a society that teaches that it's all about "me," we need to steer our teens in the right direction. When God's Word becomes their joy and heart's delight, they will learn not only to think of themselves, but also how they can serve others.

• • • • • • • • • •

*"Nobody ever outgrows Scripture; the book widens
and deepens with our years."*
—CHARLES H. SPURGEON, FROM *HEROES OF THE FAITH*

PRAYER: Lord, let ___ see the reliability of Your Word
when (he/she) lets it into (his/her) heart.
Help (him/her) to know that You have the power
to move mountains if we will only believe.
In Jesus' name, amen.

*Your word is a lamp to my feet and
a light for my path.*
—PSALM 119:105

What experiences have you had when this was true?

Teens often think with their hearts and not their minds, but they need both kinds of understanding. Knowing the ammunition that the Word provides and how to use it will give them great power and confidence when their time of need arises.

• • • • • • • • • •

*"Psalms: a 'Little Bible' since it contains,
set out in the briefest and most beautiful form,
all that is to be found in the whole Bible."*
—MARTIN LUTHER, FROM *HEROES OF THE FAITH*

PRAYER: Lord, help ___ to see You as a trusted leader
and guide, to know that Your Word is more powerful
than anything else we can say or do, and to rely on
You for the strength needed to follow You with all
(his/her) heart. In Jesus' name, amen.

Blessed are they who keep his statutes and seek him with all their heart.
—PSALM 119:2

Does this verse make you feel relieved or pressured?

Teens are very much into their rights. Validate positive behavior with certain privileges and ways of doing things that satisfy that need. As long as it won't hinder the rest of the family, this will allow them to feel that they have some control without stepping over the boundaries you have established.

• • • • • • • • • •

"I never knew all there was in the Bible until I spent those years in jail. I was constantly finding new treasures."
—JOHN BUNYAN, FROM *HEROES OF THE FAITH*

> PRAYER: Lord, keep ___ on course and committed to doing the right thing. Let (him/her) feel the Holy Spirit tug at (his/her) heart when crossing a line or thinking of doing so. Keep (his/her) eyes set on You. In Jesus' name, amen.

"... but the word of the LORD stands forever." And this is the word that was preached to you.
—1 PETER 1:25

The world changes, but God's Word doesn't. How do you feel about that?

In this ever-changing world, each teen has to decide who he or she is. Knowing who God is will help your teen to see what to strive for. The WWJD attitude can never go too far or mean enough for us as we go through life always looking to Him as an example.

• • • • • • • • • •

"The Bible without the Holy Spirit is a sundial by moonlight."
—DWIGHT L. MOODY, FROM *PATCHES OF GODLIGHT*

PRAYER: Lord, let ___ think about (his/her) future
and that choices made now will greatly affect the rest
of (his/her) life. Provide foresight into the repercus-
sions (his/her) actions will have as (he/she) lives a life
for You. In Jesus' name, amen.

For the word of God is living and active.
Sharper than any double-edged sword, it penetrates
even to dividing soul and spirit, joints and marrow;
it judges the thoughts and attitudes of the heart.
—HEBREWS 4:12

How does a "living and active" Word of God affect you day by day?

Disrespectful attitudes are often an issue with teens. Learning what is normal teen stuff versus what are real struggles will help you to know how seriously to take their moods. Teens can be leading what seems to be an admirable life, but the Evil One is always there to trip us up. We need to be always alert, on guard for the prowling lion.

• • • • • • • • • • •

"But words are things, and a small drop of ink,
falling like dew upon a thought, produces that which
makes thousands, perhaps millions, think."
—LORD BYRON, FROM *PATCHES OF GODLIGHT*

PRAYER: Lord, help ___ to prioritize what is really
important in (his/her) life. Help (him/her) to know
that not all things are as they seem in this world,
where money and affluence are the priorities, and
that it's You, always You, who need to come first in
our lives. In Jesus' name, amen.

Week 10
HUMBLE

 DAY 1	*My sheep listen to my voice; I know them,* *and they follow me.* —JOHN 10:27

Who do you listen to when you need guidance? Why?

What it means to walk humbly can be very unclear during the teen years. Knowing what is right can become clouded by peer pressure, and the allure of all the temptations they face can cause them to slip.

• • • • • • • • • • •

" . . . to reach the port of heaven we must sail sometimes
with the wind and sometimes against it—but we must sail,
and not drift, nor lie at anchor."
—OLIVER WENDELL HOLMES, FROM *PATCHES OF GODLIGHT*

> PRAYER: Lord, let ___ hear Your voice in times of
> temptation. Please remind (him/her) that (he/she)
> needs to be an example to others of what You expect
> us to be. Let ___'s actions and words be of You and
> not of the world. In Jesus' name, amen.

Therefore, if anyone is in Christ, he is a new creation; the old has gone, the new has come!
—2 CORINTHIANS 5:17

Do you find it hard to be humble?

For teens to understand the meaning of what they do is just as important as the act itself. To give up pride and let others take the lead and get the attention or the credit while we step back is hard for any of us but especially in the teen environment. Remind them that in God's eyes they are cherished for this type of attitude.

• • • • • • • • • • •

"Ring the bells that still can ring, forget your perfect offering. There is a crack in everything. That's how the light gets in."
—LEONARD COHEN, FROM *POETRY CONNECTION*

PRAYER: Lord, let ____ always go to You to seek mercy and know that (he/she) is forgiven, no matter what the sin. Help (him/her) to never feel that (he/she) has gone too far or sinned too badly to come to You, Lord. In Jesus' name, amen.

Better to be lowly in spirit and among the oppressed than to share plunder with the proud.
—PROVERBS 16:19

Can you think of a time when it was really hard for you to be one of those who had less than others around you?

Teens need to feel accepted even when their peers reject them. It's hard to be the one who goes without or is unable to do things their peers can. Learning their place in the world can be difficult, but help your teen to know where the greatest reward lies, and encourage him or her to make that their goal.

• • • • • • • • • • •

"The battle to keep up appearances unnecessarily,
the mask—whatever name you give creeping perfectionism—
robs us of our energies."
—ROBIN WORTHINGTON, FROM *PATCHES OF GODLIGHT*

PRAYER: Lord, help ___ to appreciate what (he/she)
has and not covet what others have. No matter
how much (he/she) wants someone's attention
or to have what another has, remind (him/her)
of the greatest passion (he/she) can receive, Lord:
You. In Jesus' name, amen.

DAY 4

Once more the humble will rejoice in the LORD;
the needy will rejoice in the Holy One of Israel.
—ISAIAH 29:19

Would you consider yourself to be humble?

Teens need to be reminded that being humble increases the feeling of being okay, not the opposite. The world turns things around and makes us feel that material things are what's important. Try to help them see that material possessions don't last but relationships do. This is a mature attitude toward which we should encourage our teens.

• • • • • • • • • • •

"If we have not quiet minds, outward comfort will do no more for
us than a golden slipper on a gouty foot."
—JOHN BUNYAN, FROM *HEROES OF THE FAITH*

PRAYER: Lord, let ___ see the good in being
unassuming. Show (him/her) how attractive it is
to be with someone who holds You as their greatest
possession and not the lusts of this world.
In Jesus' name, amen.

**Day
5**

*"Blessed are the poor in spirit, for theirs
is the kingdom of heaven."*
—Matthew 5:3

**What does "poor in spirit" mean to you? Do you see the need
to be poor in spirit?**

It's encouraging to know that Jesus says that, in effect, "feeling
down to earth" is blessed. If we can point out to our teens the
people they enjoy being with the most and why, they might figure out on their own what Christ is saying here.

• • • • • • • • • • •

*"God strengthens me to bear myself that heaviest weight
of all to bear inalienable weight of care."*
—Christina Rossetti, from *Patches of Godlight*

> Prayer: Lord, let ___ see the benefit in doing
> good. Help (him/her) to truly empathize
> with those who are in need. Give (him/her)
> the desire to do what is right in Your eyes
> and to understand that those who are poor
> in spirit are Your people. In Jesus' name, amen.

**Day
6**

*The Lord knows how to rescue godly men
from trials and to hold the unrighteous
for the day of judgment, while continuing
their punishment.*
—2 Peter 2:9b

Do you believe the Lord is by your side in all situations?

We can help our teens to remember that God will rescue us,
that He is the all-powerful God who can do anything if we
only have the faith to believe that He can.

• • • • • • • • • • •

*"Many times I have a knot in my stomach as I look
at the things I have said 'yes' to, and wonder just how
on earth it is all going to get done."*
—JILL BRISCOE, FROM *GOD'S FRONT DOOR*

PRAYER: Lord, enable ___ to ask for Your help during
times of hardship, to know that You are the one true
God and that nothing is impossible with You. Give
(him/her) supernatural faith and confidence in You.
In Jesus' name, amen.

*Know that the LORD has set apart the godly
for himself; the Lord will hear when I call to him.*
—PSALM 4:3

Do you always remember that you have been set apart by God for Himself?

God has a safe place set aside for us. We are precious in His
eyes, and He will provide a secure haven when we call out
to Him. For teens to know that they are set apart for God and
that He hears them when they call out to Him will provide
confidence and peace when they feel they have nowhere else
to turn.

• • • • • • • • • • •

*"Those who are pressing into the kingdom of God have a
disposition of heart to do everything that is required,
and that lies in their power to do, and to continue in it.
They have not only earnestness, but steadiness of resolution:
They do not seek with a wavering unsteady heart,
by turns or fits being off and on; but it is the constant bent
of the soul, if possible, to obtain the kingdom of God."*
—JONATHAN EDWARDS, FROM *HEROES OF THE FAITH*

PRAYER: Lord, help ___ to feel accepted always by You and never to feel that (he/she) has been sent away from You and Your mercy. Take _____ to Your hiding place when (he/she) is weary and revive (him/her) to forge ahead in obedience to You. In Jesus' name, amen.

Week 11
CHOICE

*Be strong and very courageous. Be careful
to obey all the law my servant Moses gave you;
do not turn from it to the right or to the left,
that you may be successful wherever you go . . .
But if serving the LORD seems undesirable to you,
then choose for yourselves this day whom you will
serve, whether the gods your forefathers served
beyond the River, or the gods of the Amorites,
in whose land you are living. But as for me and
my household, we will serve the LORD.*
—JOSHUA 1:7; 24:15

**Have you made the choice to serve the Lord? If so, what do
you think He will have you do?**

The abundance of material possessions makes it harder for
teens to choose the Lord. The Evil One knows what will
entice us and lead us astray. We need to constantly make our
teens aware of Satan's trap.

• • • • • • • • • • •

*"God never gives strength for tomorrow or the next hour,
but only for the strain of the minute."*
—OSWALD CHAMBERS, FROM *PATCHES OF GODLIGHT*

PRAYER: Lord, give ___ the wisdom to know
what You choose for (him/her). Keep (him/her)
constantly aware of Satan's traps.
In Jesus' name, amen.

DAY
2

*Make level paths for your feet and
take only ways that are firm.*
—PROVERBS 4:26

**Do you ever feel like you're always going uphill? Is it okay to
stop and take a rest, or should you keep going until you reach
the top? How do you know when you've reached the top?**

Teens desire excitement they may not always see on the level
path. Crossing the line by a little at first may be just enough
to encourage them to go further. But through prayer and experience, they will develop good judgment that will lead them
back to the safe and level playing field.

• • • • • • • • • •

"The fool wonders. The wise man asks."
—BENJAMIN DISRAELI, FROM *PATCHES OF GODLIGHT*

PRAYER: Lord, encourage ___ to continue to work
hard to do (his/her) best. Help (him/her) not to be
discouraged by setbacks, but in turn look to You for
strength. In Jesus' name, amen.

DAY
3

*Do not swerve to the right or the left;
keep your foot from evil.*
—PROVERBS 4:27

**Do you feel yourself swerving off the path? Who is steering
your life?**

Teens are exposed to many exciting things that entice them from God's path. Experiencing the rewards of taking the road less traveled will help them to remember what they are striving for and see where God is leading them.

● ● ● ● ● ● ● ● ● ●

"We choose our joys and sorrows long before we experience them."
—KAHLIL GIBRAN, FROM *QUOTE WORLD*

PRAYER: Lord, ___ is your child. Help (him/her) to stay on the path of righteousness, to know (he/she) will mess up at times, but that you will forgive without ever turning Your back when (he/she) turns to You. In Jesus' name, amen.

No one can serve two masters. Either he will hate the one and love the other, or he will be devoted to the one and despise the other. You cannot serve both God and Money.
—MATTHEW 6:24

As you look around at your community, do you see how money could be considered an idol?

Through TV, movies, rewards for popularity, and more, our society constantly presents other masters to guide our teens. Seek to give them clear vision so they know where they stand and will be able to make good choices.

● ● ● ● ● ● ● ● ● ●

"There is a God-shaped vacuum in the heart of every man which cannot be filled by any created thing, but only by God, the Creator, made known through Jesus Christ."
—BLAISE PASCAL, FROM *THINKEXIST QUOTES*

PRAYER: Lord, help ___ prioritize what is really important: You. Remind (him/her) that You are first in everything and that if (he/she) doesn't stand on solid Rock, (he/she) may fall for anything. In Jesus' name, amen.

DAY
5

"He who is not with me is against me, and he who does not gather with me, scatters.
—LUKE 11:23

Are you gathering with the Lord or scattering?

It's hard for teens to grasp the concept that the choices they make will make them weak or strong and that they can find strength in the Lord when their heart is feeble. As parents we need to make sure they are familiar with God's Word, which will guide them in making choices that keep them strong.

• • • • • • • • • • •

"I am seeking, I am striving, with all my heart."
—VINCENT VAN GOGH, FROM *FAMOUS QUOTES AND AUTHORS*

PRAYER: Lord, always let ___ know You are with and not not against (him/her). Help (him/her) build a life to be proud of—a happy life with You in the center. In Jesus' name, amen.

DAY
6

It is for freedom that Christ has set us free. Stand firm, then, and do not let yourselves be burdened again by a yoke of slavery.
—GALATIANS 5:1

Can you imagine being a slave to something because of what you believe in? In a sense, aren't we slaves to God?

It may be hard for teens to see that the enjoyable or exciting things they desire are not always good for them. What they think will bring them pleasure may be the very thing that binds them. Remind them of what Christ did for them on the cross to free them of their sin to live again for Him.

• • • • • • • • • • •

"Once a man is united to God how could he not
live forever? Once a man is separated from God,
what can he do but wither and die?"
—C. S. LEWIS, FROM *HEROES OF THE FAITH*

PRAYER: Lord, help ___ to speak, through You, with all Your wisdom and not feel overwhelmed or unworthy, and when there is nothing else to say, to just say thank you. In Jesus' name, amen.

DAY
7

This day I call heaven and earth as witnesses
against you that I have set before you life and death,
blessings and curses. Now choose life, so that
you and your children may live.
—DEUTERONOMY 30:19

What do you think about God giving you choices about how to live your life? Would you rather He made all your choices for you? What would that life be like?

Because teens primarily live for the moment, they may need to develop maturity before they can make this choice on their own. Sometimes teens get so caught up in their day-to-day lives that they push God out. Help them to remember to keep God first.

• • • • • • • • • • •

"If you take too long in deciding what to do
with your life, you'll find you've done it."
—GEORGE BERNARD SHAW, FROM *365 DAY BRIGHTENERS TO WARM YOUR HOME*

PRAYER: Lord, wherever you place ___, let (him/her) embrace the circumstances and work to do Your will. Help (him/her) rearrange (his/her) priorities and put You above all else. In Jesus' name, amen.

Week 12
CONFESSION

DAY 1

Therefore I tell you that no one who is speaking by the Spirit of God says, "Jesus be cursed," and no one can say, "Jesus is LORD," except by the Holy Spirit.
—1 CORINTHIANS 12:3

Can you always tell when you've met a Christian? How do you know?

Discerning teens can tell when they have found Christian friends. Being certain of their own convictions and their faith will help them stay on the narrow path, including choosing friends wisely.

• • • • • • • • • • •

"A loving person lives in a loving world. A hostile person lives in a hostile world; everyone you meet is your mirror."
—KEN KEYES, JR., FROM PATCHES OF GODLIGHT

PRAYER: Lord, help ___ not to let a small disobedience turn into a bigger disobedience. Safeguard (him/her) against others who might lead (him/her) astray. When trouble comes, move (him/her) by the Holy Spirit to turn to You and to confess when (he/she) fails. In Jesus' name, amen.

That if you confess with your mouth, "Jesus is Lord," and believe in your heart that God raised him from the dead, you will be saved.
—Romans 10:9

Do you ever wonder if you are really saved?

It's hard for teens to get in touch with what they are feeling and discern where their heart is. The knowledge that they are sealed in Christ will comfort them when they feel uncertain.

• • • • • • • • • • •

*"Oh Spirit, descend plentifully into my heart.
Enlighten the dark corners of this neglected dwelling
and scatter there the cheerful beams."*
—St. Augustine, from *Brainy Quote*

PRAYER: Lord, let ___ seek Your face to know You as (his/her) God. Encourage (him/her) to lean on you during times of doubt and despair, turmoil and weakness, when the Evil One taunts (him/her) with lies. In Jesus' name, amen.

As the Scripture says, "Anyone who trusts in him will never be put to shame."
—Romans 10:11

Do you trust God?

Trying to fit in with their peers can lead teens astray. Knowing God will never shame us is an incredible comfort. Remind teens that God hears them when they call to Him and that to turn to Him in confession and repentance is to find refuge.

• • • • • • • • • • •

"We trust, not because a God exists, but because this God exists."
—C. S. Lewis, from *Heroes of the Faith*

PRAYER: Lord, help ___ to always know that (he/she) can come to you in repentance and confess (his/her) sins. No matter what darkness or fear (he/she) experiences, let (him/her) feel You wash over (him/her) with refreshing waters. In Jesus' name, amen.

DAY
4

Fix your thoughts on Jesus, the apostle and high priest whom we confess.
—HEBREWS 3:1B

Have you ever felt lead to share scripture with someone?

Reminding teens of favorite verses can steady them in difficult times. When they rely on God instead on themselves, they will find the confidence to respond wisely to their peers' questions about their faith.

• • • • • • • • • •

A wise man will make more opportunities than he finds."
—FRANCIS BACON, FROM *PATCHES OF GODLIGHT*

PRAYER: Lord, thank You for giving ___ Your words to guide (him/her). Help us to read and memorize Your Word so we can in turn share it with others. In Jesus' name, amen.

DAY
5

Whosoever therefore shall confess me before men, him will I confess also before my Father which is in heaven.
—MATTHEW 10:22

Have you confessed Jesus? Why or why not?

The reassurance teens find in knowing that they have been sealed with Christ in baptism is glorious to witness. Encourage your teen to share this experience with other believers so he or she can be held accountable and can become an example to nonbelievers as well.

• • • • • • • • • • •

*"There is nothing that wearies you more
than a complaining spirit.*
—JILL BRISCOE, FROM *GOD'S FRONT DOOR*

> PRAYER: Lord, let ___ see confessing Jesus brings (him/her) closer to You. Help ___ to want to live out (his/her) faith by showing others how important You are to (him/her). In Jesus' name, amen.

DAY
6

*I tell you, whoever acknowledges me before men,
the Son of Man will also acknowledge him
before the angels of God.*
—LUKE 12:8

Have you ever denied Christ?

For many teens making the grade in school or with peers isn't easy. There may be a time when it was hard for them to acknowledge God publicly and they failed. Let them know that when they come to God in repentance, He will forgive their weakness and help them to move forward in faith.

• • • • • • • • • • •

"Every saint has a past and every sinner has a future."
—SIXTEENTH-CENTURY POET, FROM *PATCHES OF GODLIGHT*

> PRAYER: Lord, keep ___ strong for you. Bless and make (him/her) Yours. Make (his/her) life count and help (him/her) serve You with words and deeds. In Jesus' name, amen.

DAY 7

Whoever acknowledges me before men, I will also acknowledge him before my Father in heaven.
—MATTHEW 10:32

What would it be like to be acknowledged before God?

Giving of themselves is hard for teens who are absorbed with self-preservation. When their day is full of temptations or they have been wronged by others, encourage them to forgive those who have hurt them and also to confess and seek God's forgiveness if they have behaved poorly.

• • • • • • • • • •

*"Confession is good for the conscience,
but it usually bypasses the soul."*
—MIGNON MCLAUGHLIN, FROM *THE NEUROTIC'S NOTEBOOK*

PRAYER: Lord, give ___ the courage to confess you before (his/her) peers. Pour out Your blessings on (him/her). Give (him/her) the strength to live a life that is pleasing in Your eyes and to love others the way You love. In Jesus' name, amen.

Week 13

FRIENDS

*A friend loves at all times, and a brother
is born for adversity.*
—Proverbs 17:17

Do you feel closer to your friends than to your siblings?

Saying no to peer pressure is difficult. Knowing they have permission to say no can help, but teens still need to develop the confidence to follow through. Having a circle of godly friends can make all the difference in whether a teen stands strong against peer pressure or gives in to it.

• • • • • • • • • •

*"Real friendship is shown in times of trouble;
prosperity is full of friends."*
—Abraham Kuyper, from *Patches of Godlight*

PRAYER: Lord, help our family to continue to support one another. Even if we don't know everything our teen is going through, You do, and we trust in You to watch over (him/her) and guide (him/her) in Your ways. In Jesus' name, amen.

A man of many companions may come to ruin, but there is a friend who sticks closer than a brother.
—PROVERBS 18:24

Do you have a wide circle of friends or a few close friends?

If your child has good, close friends, he or she is fortunate. Encourage those relationships and help your teen through rough spots when disagreements come up between them. Guide your teen in learning how to be a good friend. Being a good friend attracts good friends.

• • • • • • • • • • •

*"Oh, the comfort, the inexpressible comfort
of feeling safe with a person: having neither
to weigh thoughts nor measure words, but to pour
them out. Just as they are—chaff and grain together,
knowing that a faithful hand will take and sift them,
keep what is worth keeping, and then with the
breath of kindness, blow the rest away."*
—GEORGE ELIOT, FROM PATCHES OF GODLIGHT

PRAYER: Lord, help ___ discern which friends will always be there for them and which ones will let (him/her) down. Open (his/her) eyes to see the real person beneath the outward appearance.
In Jesus' name, amen.

As iron sharpens iron, so one man sharpens another.
—PROVERBS 27:17

Think about a time when you sharpened a friend or a friend sharpened you.

When teens don't feel they can confide in family members or friends, a good therapist who specializes in working with teens can help them to develop coping skills. Professional counseling has fewer stigmas nowadays than it did in the past, so teens who need help can receive it without being judged by their peers.

● ● ● ● ● ● ● ● ● ● ●

"When two go together, one of them at least looks forward to see what is best; a man by himself, though he be careful, still has less mind in him than two, and his wits have less weight."
—HOMER, FROM *PATCHES OF GODLIGHT*

PRAYER: Lord, equip ___ to sharpen (his/her) friends and to accept the ways others sharpen (him/her). Let (his/her) friends be kind enough to tell ___ when (he/she) falters and to lift (him/her) up. Help ___ to do the same for others.

DAY 4

Two are better than one, because they have a good return for their work: If one falls down, his friend can help him up. But pity the man who falls and has no one to help him up!
—ECCLESIASTES 4:9-11

Which of your friends would do for you what this verse says?

Truancy and skipping class are tempting and common. It sounds fun. What can it hurt to miss one class? Getting away with it once usually leads to a second and a third time, however, and can lead to other offenses that are more serious. A circle of godly friends can help teens to resist temptation and help him or her up after a fall.

● ● ● ● ● ● ● ● ● ● ●

"Friendship doubles our joys and halves our grief."
—SWEDISH PROVERB, FROM *PATCHES OF GODLIGHT*

PRAYER: Lord, enable ___ to gather around (him/her)
others who share Your mission. Let those who
are strong willed and not fearful of standing alone
surround (him/her) in times of trial and temptation.
Let (him/her) be that example to others when
the need arises. In Jesus' name, amen.

DAY 5

Though one may be overpowered,
two can defend themselves. A cord of three
strands is not quickly broken.
—ECCLESIASTES 4:12

How can friends be a good influence or a bad influence?

Teens can easily be made to feel that they don't have the
strength to stand up to others. This creates low self-esteem
and makes them a target for bullies. As parents we can help our
teens learn to project confidence when they face tough situations. Having friends they can depend on for support provides
even more strength when dealing with bullies.

• • • • • • • • • • •

If you have a friend worth loving,
Love him. Yes, and let him know
That you love him, ere life's evening
Tinge his brow with sunset glow.
Why should good words ne'er be said
Of a friend—till he is dead?
—ALEXANDER MACLEOD, FROM *PATCHES OF GODLIGHT*

PRAYER: Lord, lead ___ to other teens who
will be a positive influence in (his/her) life.
Draw others near who will lift (him/her) up.
In Jesus' name, amen.

DAY 6

Do two walk together unless they have agreed to do so?
—AMOS 3:3

Have you ever felt as if you were walking together with some-one, only to discover later that the other person wasn't really walking with you?

Good friends can help pull teens away from trouble. When your child is the one making the wrong choices, pray that they have made sound choices about the friends they are with. As much as we want our child to be the leader, sometimes it takes a confident friend to lead them in the right direction.

• • • • • • • • • •

"Think what a better world it would be if we all, the whole world, had cookies and milk about three o'clock every afternoon and then lay down with our blankies for a nap. Or if all governments had a basic policy to always put things back where they found them and to clean up after their own mess."
—ROBERT FULGHUM, FROM *ALL I REALLY NEEDED TO KNOW I LEARNED IN KINDERGARTEN*

PRAYER: Lord, help ___ to find trustworthy friends that (he/she) can pour (his/her) heart out to, not just someone to spend time with, but a friend (he/she) can confide in who has a heart that longs for You. In Jesus' name, amen.

DAY 7

Greater love has no one than this, that he lay down his life for his friends.
—JOHN 15:13

Think of someone in your life you believe would love you in this way. Who would you actually give your life for?

The Internet overloads teens with information. There are many temptations on the Net, and a teen's judgment can easily be clouded. Keeping a close eye on how much time your teen spends using the computer, cell phone, or other device can help you know what he or she is being exposed to. Guarding our teens from harmful influences even when they resist our authority is an expression of our sacrificial love for them.

• • • • • • • • • • •

"He is your friend who pushes you closer to God."
—ABRAHAM KUYPER, FROM *PATCHES OF GODLIGHT*

PRAYER: Lord, help ___ to be wise about whom (he/she) chooses to follow. Help (him/her) to be a good example for others by keeping You as the focus in every relationship.
In Jesus' name, amen.

Week 14

HOLY

*You are to be holy to me because I, the Lord,
am holy, and I have set you apart from the
nations to be my own.*
—LEVITICUS 20:26

If this verse is true, how are you holy?

It is so important for teens to feel they are chosen by God. As they make their relationship with Him the first and foremost thing in their life, the right earthly relationships will follow.

• • • • • • • • • • •

*"It is not a question of our equipment
but of our poverty, not of what we bring with us,
but of what God puts into us."*
—ABRAHAM KUYPER, FROM *PATCHES OF GODLIGHT*

PRAYER: Lord, guide ____ to be wise in (his/her)
decisions and stay clean. Let (him/her) feel the
cleansing that only You can give. And once (he/she)
knows this purity, let (him/her) want it always.
In Jesus' name, amen.

You and your children return to the LORD your God and obey him with all your heart and with all your soul according to everything I command you today.
—DEUTERONOMY 30:2

To what or whom have you given your heart and soul?

Whatever is important to teens will control their lives. There are so many temptations that can lead them astray and scramble their priorities. Make it your priority to get them plugged into church. From choir to missions, help them to find their niche.

• • • • • • • • • •

*"I am never better than when I am
on the full stretch for God."*
—GEORGE WHITEFIELD, FROM HIS *JOURNAL*

PRAYER: Lord, let ___ always see You as worthy of (his/her) entire heart and soul. Don't let the Evil One cover (his/her) eyes and ears so (he/she) can't see and hear Your truth. Let (his/her) path always lead to You. In Jesus' name, amen.

He has showed you, O man, what is good. And what does the LORD require of you? To act justly and to love mercy and to walk humbly with your God.
—MICAH 6:8

Do you feel it's easier to make the choices described in this verse or the opposite?

Knowing what causes stress for your teen will allow you to help him or her with tough choices. We all have weaknesses, and as parents we need to pinpoint what might tempt our teen so we can intervene before he or she experiences harm.

• • • • • • • • • •

*"God sends no one away empty except those
who are full of themselves."*
—DWIGHT L. MOODY, FROM *THE MOODY INDEX*

PRAYER: Lord, bring ___ back to You when (he/she)
strays. Help (him/her) learn from mistakes so
(he/she) can become stronger in You and not depend
on things of the world. In Jesus' name, amen.

DAY
4

*Therefore, there is now no condemnation
for those who are in Christ Jesus.*
—ROMANS 8:1

When do you feel condemned?

Teens often feel picked on or oppressed, sometimes because
they don't fit in with the crowd or because of their faith.
Help them by your example to be confident in their beliefs when
others put them down.

• • • • • • • • • • •

*"I thought back to the time when my hungering heart
and malnourished, empty spirit wondered silently
if they would ever experience a dawn chorus,"*
—JILL BRISCOE, FROM *GOD'S FRONT DOOR*

PRAYER: Lord, lead ___ along Your narrow path
and in Your ways. Help (him/her) recognize
when (he/she) is nearing the edge, and give
(him/her) the strength to veer back to the middle
again. Let (him/her) feel Your gentle nudge
of encouragement that (he/she) is doing
what is right. In Jesus' name, amen.

DAY

5

Therefore, get rid of all moral filth and the evil that is so prevalent and humbly accept the word planted in you, which can save you.
—JAMES 1:21

God has provided a way to live a pure life. What is your part?

Purity goes much further than sex. It extends to teens' entire lives. Feeling good about themselves will help them to stay pure. Feeling accepted by peers and finding their place in the world will help to keep them from doing something they know is wrong just to fit in.

• • • • • • • • • • •

"O thou Light of lights, keep us from inward darkness, grant us so to sleep in peace that we may arise to work according to thy will."
—LANCELOT ANDREWS, FROM *AN EVENING COMMENDATION*

PRAYER: Lord, continue to encourage ____ to come to You when (he/she) needs to be cleansed. Let (him/her) know that Your grace is enough, that (he/she) is forgiven before ever asking, and that (he/she) is white as snow in Your eyes. In Jesus' name, amen.

DAY

6

Finally, brothers, whatever is true, whatever is noble, whatever is right, whatever is pure, whatever is lovely, whatever is admirable— if anything is excellent or praiseworthy— think about such things.
—PHILIPPIANS 4:8

What makes you feel loved?

Help teens to see the positive things instead of only the negative. They can become overwhelmed and feel as if everything in their lives is under attack. The devil knows our weaknesses, but the Lord knows our strengths. Remind your teens of theirs and help them to focus on what is lovely, admirable, excellent, and praiseworthy.

• • • • • • • • • • •

"Our greatest glory is not in never falling,
but in getting up every time we do."
—CONFUCIUS, FROM *QUOTATIONS IN CULTURE AND HUMANITIES*

PRAYER: Lord, keep ___'s thoughts on You and on what is excellent in Your eyes. Teach (him/her) what You want of (him/her) and how to succeed in life by glorifying You. In Jesus' name, amen.

DAY 7

Have mercy on me, O LORD, for I am weak;
Heal me, O LORD, for my bones are troubled.
My soul also is greatly troubled;
But You, O LORD—how long?
Return, O LORD, deliver me!
Oh, save me for Your mercy's sake!
—PSALMS 6:24 NKJV

Do you walk in the light?

Vulgar language is a part of the everyday life of teens. It's found in music, movies, books, and conversation. Helping teens to identify their feelings when they indulge in these types of negative behaviors can help them know when to stop and what they need to look for as an alternative.

• • • • • • • • • • •

"The wicked flee when no one pursues;
but the righteous are bold as a lion."
—PROVERBS 28:1 (WEB)

PRAYER: Lord, don't let ___ go toward
the darkness but keep (him/her) in the light.
Expose Satan and his evil ways and teach
___ how to protect (himself/herself)
with Your Word, prayer, and the Holy Spirit.
In Jesus' name, amen.

Week 15
JOY

DAY
1

A joyful heart is good medicine.
—Proverbs 17:22 NASB

How has this verse been true for you?

Knowing how to feel joy through God is different from the happiness we find in the world. Help your teen to identify the difference. The joy that comes from knowing God may not seem as intense as the temporary joy of this earth, but God's joy is everlasting.

• • • • • • • • • • •

"Those who bring sunshine to the lives of others
cannot keep it from themselves."
—James M. Barrie, from *Patches of Godlight*

PRAYER: Lord, enlarge ___'s understanding to know that You are the ultimate good feeling. Let (him/her) discover You in what makes (him/her) happy in this world. In Jesus' name, amen.

DAY
2

You have filled my heart with greater joy.
—PSALM 4:7

How could this verse help you at times when you are not joyful?

If teens learn to trust that their joy will return, they will not lose hope as so many do. Teens don't always look past the moment they are in. To look for the power that only God can give will help them cling to what is good.

• • • • • • • • • • •

"The days that make us happy make us wise."
—JOHN MANSFIELD, FROM *PATCHES OF GODLIGHT*

PRAYER: Lord, let the Holy Spirit guide ___
in learning how to find inner peace through You.
Let it become automatic that (he/she) seeks You
during times of trouble. Teach (him/her) to depend
wholly on You. In Jesus' name, amen.

DAY
3

Let us sing for joy to the LORD!
—PSALM 95:1

Do you sometimes take your faith so seriously that you can't enjoy your relationship with God?

Worship is a joyful celebration focused on God. When teens feel confident enough to worship freely, their souls will also be freed.

• • • • • • • • • • •

*"Into all our lives, in many simple, familiar,
homely ways, God infuses this element of joy from the
surprises of life, which unexpectedly brighten our days,
and fill our eyes with light."*
—SAMUEL LONGFELLOW, FROM *365 DAY BRIGHTENERS TO WARM YOUR HOME*

PRAYER: Lord, help ___ to live out (his/her)
relationship with You as if with a friend. Let
(him/her) know You understand (him/her) and
feel what (he/she) feels. In Jesus' name, amen.

So do not fear, for I am with you;
do not be dismayed, for I am your God.
I will strengthen you and help you; I will
uphold you with my righteous right hand.
—ISAIAH 41:10

Can you tell Christians from those who are not?

Teens need to know that being Christian doesn't necessarily mean life will be easier. And just because someone claims to be a Christian doesn't mean he or she will always act like one. None of us do all the time. We are to show forgiveness and grace to others just as God showers them on us.

• • • • • • • • • •

"The deeper that sorrow carves into your being, the more joy
you can contain. Is not the cup that holds your wine
the very cup that was burned in the potter's oven?"
—KAHLIL GIBRAN, FROM *WISDOM QUOTES*

PRAYER: Lord, help ___ to hold on to (his/her)
true self and not let go. Build (him/her) up
to be like You in forgiveness and love.
Let (him/her) overlook the blemishes of others
and work on (his/her) own transgressions.
In Jesus' name, amen.

DAY
5

The LORD has done great things for us,
and we are filled with joy.
—PSALM 126:3

Why are our hearts not always filled with joy?

Remind your teen that the highs and the lows of life will give the joyful times more meaning. Developing the confidence that the lows will pass will help teens to endure in situations when things seem wrong or unjust. There will always be people who are unfair, but to know that God is always just provides great comfort and joy.

• • • • • • • • • •

"The joy of brightening other lives, bearing
each other's burden, easing others' loads and
supplanting empty hearts and lives with
generous gifts becomes for us the magic . . . "
—W. C. JONES, FROM *FAMOUS QUOTES AND QUOTATIONS*

PRAYER: Lord, enable ____ to experience the joy that only You bring. Let (him/her) see that true joy comes from You, and only You. In Jesus' name, amen.

DAY
6

Be joyful always.
—1 THESSALONIANS 5:16

Is it possible to always be joyful? If not, why does the scripture say to do it?

We need to teach teens what is most important to strive for in life. Admonish them to be realistic about what they can expect from themselves, but encourage them not to settle for less than their best efforts. Help them to recognize that true joy is found in achieving their highest goals, knowing they are doing it for God.

• • • • • • • • • •

*"God is most glorified in us
when we are most satisfied in Him."*
—JOHN PIPER, FROM *THINKEXIST QUOTES*

PRAYER: Lord, empower ____ to seek after Your joyful
ways and to truly experience through You the life
You want us to live. In Jesus' name, amen.

DAY	
7	

You will fill me with joy in your presence.
—PSALM 16:11

How does this verse answer yesterday's question?

Knowing that God is always available to us provides great power. When teens take this to heart and carry it with them during times of trouble, they develop courage, confidence, and true joy.

• • • • • • • • • • •

"Peace is seeing a sunset and knowing who to thank."
—ANONYMOUS

PRAYER: Lord, make ____ aware of Your
constant presence. Keep (him/her) safe in Your
loving embrace. Let (him/her) fear nothing,
knowing that You are always beside (him/her).
In Jesus' name, amen.

Week 16
PEACE

You will keep in perfect peace him whose mind is steadfast, because he trusts in you.
—Isaiah 26:3

Why do you think there are times when you're not in perfect peace?

Trusting in ourselves is self-confidence. Trusting in the Lord is faith. Showing teens how much more powerful faith is than self-confidence will increase the faith they already have. As they learn to trust God with both their heart and their head, they will experience perfect peace.

• • • • • • • • • • •

"Be careful to preserve your health. It is a trick of the devil, which he employs to deceive good souls, to incite them to do more than they are able, in order that they may no longer be able to do anything."
—Vincent de Paul, from *365 Day Brighteners to Warm Your Home*

> PRAYER: Lord, let ___ desire to be steadfast and trust completely in You. Help (his/her) faith never to falter, to be unwavering in (his/her) life, not only to secure (his/her) own spirit but as an example to others. In Jesus' name, amen.

DAY 2

The Lord blesses his people with peace.
—PSALM 29:11

What do we have to do to receive the Lord's blessing of peace?

No matter what happens, God's peace is always available for us. That's an amazing thought if we really drink it in. To have peace from the Lord is so big we can't grasp it, but just think what it would be like if we didn't have it. This is what makes us count our blessings.

• • • • • • • • • •

*"Every man has in himself a continent
of undiscovered character. Happy is he who acts
the Columbus to his own soul."*
—SIR J. STEPHEN, FROM *MEDITATIONS FOR PARENTS WHO DO TOO MUCH*

> PRAYER: Lord, don't let others rob ___ of the peace You offer. Let (him/her) grasp this and run to You, not looking back. In Jesus' name, amen.

DAY 3

And the peace of God, which transcends all understanding, will guard over your hearts and your minds in Christ Jesus.
—PHILIPPIANS 4:7

Have you ever experienced peace without understanding how you could have it under the circumstances?

It often seems that non-Christians have more fun because they don't act with the integrity God demands of believers. But the peace that comes from possessions and human relationships comes and goes, while the peace that comes from God is always there, even in difficult circumstances. This lesson is especially hard for teens to learn.

• • • • • • • • • •

"It is not my ability, but my response to God's ability, that counts."
—CORRIE TEN BOOM, FROM *HEROES OF THE FAITH*

PRAYER: Lord, let ___ live within Your all-affirming love and peace so that (he/she) can be an example to others. In Jesus' name, amen.

DAY
4

Peace I leave with you; my peace I give you.
—JOHN 14:27

Have you experienced the peace that Jesus gives?

Focusing our mind on God rather than on ourselves is often difficult, but we are rewarded with true peace when we do. Ask your teen whether he or she has ever felt God's peace. For teens to know this peace and recognize where it comes from rather than giving the credit to something else will help them to remain faithful when they are tempted.

• • • • • • • • • •

"Into thy hands, O Lord, I commend my spirit."
—CHRISTOPHER COLUMBUS, LAST WORDS

PRAYER: Lord, let ___ submit to You and find Your peace. Help (him/her) to know when You are working in (his/her) life. I pray that (he/she) is open to You and accepts Your will. In Jesus' name, amen.

DAY
5

He himself is our peace.
—EPHESIANS 2:14

How does knowing that Jesus is our peace relieve pressure from us?

We are taught to work for the material things we need, but peace with God is His gift, not something we can earn. Knowing His peace puts everything else in perspective.

• • • • • • • • • •

"Take, O Lord, and receive my entire liberty, my memory, my understanding and my whole will. All that I am and all that I possess You have given me. I surrender it all to You to be disposed of according to Your will. Give me only Your love and Your grace; with these I will be rich enough and will desire nothing more."
—IGNATIUS OF LOYOLA, FROM *PATCHES OF GODLIGHT*

PRAYER: Lord, let ___ desire You and the calm only You provide. Help (him/her) to know that You are there during the hard times and to give You credit for the good times as well. In Jesus' name, amen.

DAY
6

Peace I leave with you; my peace I give you. I do not give to you as the world gives. Do not let your hearts be troubled and do no be afraid.
—JOHN 14:27

How is the peace that comes from God different from the peace that comes from the things of the world?

The peace of the world is deceiving and short lived, especially in a teen's world. It's hard to keep up with cultural and social changes, but the assurance that God has a plan for our lives can give us the peace we need to enjoy life while we have it.

• • • • • • • • • •

"There is no pillow so soft as a clear conscience."
—FRENCH PROVERB, FROM *PATCHES OF GODLIGHT*

PRAYER: Lord, lead ___ away from strife and into
Your world of peace. Help (him/her) to know the
peace that only You can give if they'll only reach for
the prize. In Jesus' name, amen.

DAY 7

*All this is from God, who reconciled us to himself
through Christ and gave us the ministry of reconciliation.*
—2 CORINTHIANS 5:18

How can we remain in God's peace?

It's hard for teens not to get caught up in the "me" attitude of
our culture and to stay focused on God. Help your teen to
know that the reward of peace is there for them when they do.

• • • • • • • • • •

*How sweet the Name of Jesus sounds
in a believer's ear!
It soothes his sorrows, heals his wounds,
and drives away his fear."*
—JOHN NEWTON, FROM *HEROES OF THE FAITH*

PRAYER: Lord, give ___ a hunger for the peace only
You can give. Let it become a habit for (him/her)
to go to You no matter what the situation, knowing
You will be there when things of this world will not.
In Jesus' name, amen.

Week 17
INSPIRATION

DAY 1

But it is the spirit in a man, the breath of the Almighty, that gives him understanding.
—JOB 32:8

What do you find is the difference between "head learning" and "heart learning"?

Teens often think with their hearts, but they need both head and heart learning. Understanding how life works in a logical way can help them to keep things in perspective. But a tender heart is necessary for one to develop loving relationships.

• • • • • • • • • • •

"I have been tortured with longing to believe— am so, indeed, even now; and the yearning grows stronger, the more cogent the intellectual difficulties that stand in the way."
—FYODOR DOSTOYEVSKY, IN A LETTER TO A FRIEND

PRAYER: Lord, reveal to ___ both Your heart lessons and head wisdom. Let (him/her) remember how You dealt with people in situations that are similar to what (he/she) comes across. In Jesus' name, amen.

For the Holy Spirit will teach you at that time what you should say.
—LUKE 12:12

Where should you look for wisdom of speech?

Let teens speak their piece and let them hear yours. Learning to communicate respectfully with their parents will help them in their relationships with others.

• • • • • • • • • •

"Let me say I believe God will supply all my need, and then let me run dry, with no outlook, and see whether I will go through the trial of faith, or whether I will sink back to something lower."
—OSWALD CHAMBERS, FROM *SUBLIME INTIMACY*

PRAYER: Lord, help me model to ___ the patience to let the Spirit guide me in what to say. Give me Your wisdom in my answers and in knowing what is fair and what is right. In Jesus' name, amen.

But make up your mind not to worry beforehand how you will defend yourselves. For I will give you words and wisdom that none of your adversaries will be able to resist or contradict.
—LUKE 21:14-15

Do you spend time worrying about what to say, or do you prepare to receive the Lord's gift of wisdom?

Teens often encounter harsh words. Help them to learn not to accept them or to use them. Restraint can be hard when they feel they are being mistreated, but people respect the one who keeps control of his or her tongue.

• • • • • • • • • •

"Fussing always ends in sin. We imagine that a little anxiety and worry are an indication of how really wise we are; it is much

more an indication of how really wicked we are. Fretting springs from a determination to get our own way. Our Lord never worried and He was never anxious, because He was not 'out' to realize His own ideas; He was 'out' to realize God's ideas."
—OSWALD CHAMBERS, FROM *MY UTMOST FOR HIS HIGHEST*

PRAYER: Lord, let ___ be aware of Your presence when (he/she) is tempted to join in inappropriate conversations. Cause the Holy Spirit to tug at (his/her) heart when (his/her) lips become loose and (his/her) words go astray. In Jesus' name, amen.

DAY
4

All scripture is God-breathed and is useful for teaching, rebuking, correcting and training in righteousness.
—2 TIMOTHY 3:16

How could you use this scripture to help a friend?

Teens are faced with opportunities to share their faith, and they need to be equipped with knowledge of scripture. Memorizing verses is key, but regularly reading the Bible will help them keep the basics in mind so they can converse with knowledge.

• • • • • • • • • •

"Unless we form the habit of going to the Bible in bright moments as well as in trouble, we cannot fully respond to its consolations because we lack equilibrium between light and darkness."
—HELEN KELLER, FROM *BRAINY QUOTES*

PRAYER: Lord, prepare ___ with Your words to guide others to salvation. Let (him/her) also turn to the Bible for answers during times of struggle. In Jesus' name, amen.

DAY
5

And I have filled him with the Spirit of God, with skill, ability and knowledge in all kinds of crafts.
—EXODUS 31:3

Where do your skills, abilities, and knowledge come from?

As teens practice the gifts given to them by God, they develop their skills and gain confidence. Helping them to recognize and use their gifts brings God the praise and thanksgiving He deserves. We need to teach our teens to remember to thank Him for their abilities.

· · · · · · · · · · ·

"Creating new ways to look inside your spiritual self will be necessary. You can't leave this part of yourself alone. You need the energy and power."
— CARMEN WEBB, FROM *TAKING MY PLACE IN MEDICINE*

PRAYER: Lord, help ___ to remain humble about the gifts You have given to (him/her). Let (him/her) praise You for giving them freely. Teach ___ to use those gifts to do Your will. In Jesus' name, amen.

DAY
6

I will come down and speak with you there, and I will take of the Spirit that is on you and put the Spirit on them. They will help you carry the burden of the people so that you will not have to carry it alone.
—NUMBERS 11:17

How can we depend on others to help carry our burdens?

Friendships are so important to teens but can also be very challenging. Discovering who they are will lead them to individuals they feel comfortable with. If they lean on God, they will develop discernment that will guide them into the right relationships.

· · · · · · · · · · ·

"We make our friends, we make our enemies; but God makes our next door neighbor."
—G. K. CHESTERTON, FROM *PATCHES OF GODLIGHT*

> PRAYER: Lord, reveal to ___ friendships (he/she) can lean on. Help (him/her) to know who (his/her) true friends are and also (his/her) enemies so (he/she) will better know how to engage the people in (his/her) life through You. In Jesus' name, amen.

DAY
7

Your love has given me great joy and encouragement, because you, brother, have refreshed the hearts of the saints.
—PHILEMON 1:7

How does this verse help you to see that there is power available to us from God and not just from ourselves?

When teens are in the right relationships, they will discover the same kind of joy and encouragement Paul talks about in this verse. The opposite is also true. The wrong kinds of relationships can destroy their confidence and lead them astray from God's good path. Being firmly grounded in God's Word can make all the difference in the companions they choose.

· · · · · · · · · · ·

"Lay hold of something that will help you, and then use it to help somebody else."
—BOOKER T. WASHINGTON, FROM *GREAT QUOTES FROM GREAT LEADERS*

> PRAYER: Lord, help ___ to choose (his/her) companions wisely. Let them be those who will refresh (his/her) heart. In Jesus' name, amen.

Week 18
MERCY

DAY
1

May the LORD judge between you and me. And may the LORD avenge the wrongs you have done to me, but my hand will not touch you.
—1 SAMUEL 24:12

Which is easier for you, to let the Lord avenge wrongs done to you or for you to do it yourself?

Teens' pride can easily be bruised when they are faced with difficult situations. Knowing God will make the wrongs right is so important during these times. Having a Bible verse or a saying that reminds them of this when they feel they are treated unjustly can encourage them to wait for God to act.

• • • • • • • • • •

"Indeed, I tremble for my country when I reflect that God is just."
—THOMAS JEFFERSON, ON THE JEFFERSON MEMORIAL

PRAYER: Lord, help ___ to know You will avenge the wrongs done to (him/her) and to rest in that certainty. Give (him/her) patience when tested and teased, taunted and put down. Give (him/her) the strength to surrender all things to You and walk away from conflict. In Jesus' name, amen.

DAY 2

Love and faithfulness meet together;
righteousness and peace kiss each other.
—PSALM 85:10

If you don't have love, faithfulness, righteousness, and peace, what do you have?

To love is to be faithful, no matter what the circumstances. Righteousness and peace stand together. It is hard to have one without the other. This goes against the ways of the world, but what a perfect way to try to live.

• • • • • • • • • • •

"Love wholeheartedly, be surprised,
give thanks and praise, then you will discover
the fullness of your life."
—BROTHER DAVID STEINDL-RAST, FROM *PATCHES OF GODLIGHT*

PRAYER: Lord, You know what ___'s needs are.
Please help (him/her) learn to let You balance
(his/her) life. Help ___ to keep (his/her) head up and
cling to the faithful love You provide, knowing that
righteous peace is the reward.
In Jesus' name, amen.

DAY 3

Let love and faithfulness never leave you;
bind them around your neck, write them
on the tablet of your heart.
—PROVERBS 3:3

Does this verse mean that you have to make an effort to maintain love and faithfulness?

Although your teen may love the Lord, faithfulness is more difficult to maintain. Yet it is what keeps any relationship alive. Remaining faithful in our relationships ensures that they will last.

• • • • • • • • • •

"Faith goes up the stairs that love has built and looks out the window which hope has opened."
—CHARLES SPURGEON, FROM *HEROES OF THE FAITH*

PRAYER: Lord, teach ___ to love and be faithful to You and others. Yours is the ultimate relationship, perfect in every way. Help us to learn from Your example of unconditional love. In Jesus' name, amen.

DAY
4

He who despises his neighbor sins,
but blessed is he who is kind to the needy.
—PROVERBS 14:21

How should you respond to a friend or neighbor who mistreats you?

Being merciful to everyone according to Christ's example is what we strive for. Fickle friends can confuse teens, however, and make it hard for them to know who their friends really are. We are called to forgive those who hurt us, but knowing when to let go of a relationship is also sometimes necessary.

• • • • • • • • • •

"Eat with the rich, but go play with the poor,
who are capable of joy."
—L. P. SMITH, FROM *PATCHES OF GODLIGHT*

PRAYER: Lord, reveal to ___ who (his/her) real friends are and also (his/her) foes. Let (him/her) grow those relationships with true allies and have patience with those who are not. In Jesus' name, amen.

Blessed are the merciful, for they will be shown mercy.
—MATTHEW 5:7

How does it make you feel when you are merciful to someone who isn't easy to like?

In today's world, teens are bound to encounter others with different sexual preferences. They need to know what God's Word says on the subject but also leave judgment to God. Remind them to pray for others and let God guide them.

• • • • • • • • • • •

"When you carry out acts of kindness you get a wonderful feeling inside. It is as though something inside your body responds and says, yes, this is how I ought to feel."
—RABBI HAROLD KUSHNER, FROM *PATCHES OF GODLIGHT*

PRAYER: Lord, let ___ feel that it is acceptable for (him/her) to ask questions, and guide (him/her) to know and follow Your will. Help (him/her) to understand that we are all sinful and are not to judge others. Remind (him/her) that You are the Judge in all matters. In Jesus' name, amen.

But you must return to your God; maintain love and justice, and wait for your God always.
—HOSEA 12:6

Where are you when it becomes necessary for you to return to God?

Teens will be tempted to cheat in many ways. It has become acceptable to cheat to make good grades, even when they're not deserved. Reminding teens of Christ's sacrificial work on their behalf and that His will is for them to succeed with honesty will help put things back in perspective.

● ● ● ● ● ● ● ● ● ●

*"A thing long expected takes the form
of the unexpected when at last it comes."*
—MARK TWAIN, FROM MEDITATIONS FOR PARENTS WHO DO TOO MUCH

PRAYER: Lord, let ___ always act with honor and
self-respect in making hard choices. Help (him/her)
to turn to You when temptation strikes
and to remember and observe Your ways.
In Jesus' name, amen.

| DAY 7 | *He who pursues righteousness and love finds life, prosperity, and honor.* —PROVERBS 21:21 |

What would pursuing righteousness and love look like in real life?

Judging others is the norm for teens, deciding who is in and who is out. If our teens would engage others with acceptance, what a great example they would be, not only for their peers, but also for adults.

● ● ● ● ● ● ● ● ● ●

*"Look around the habitable world, how few know
their own good, or knowing it, pursue."*
—JOHN DRYDEN, FROM PATCHES OF GODLIGHT

PRAYER: Lord, let ___ strive for reconciliation where
there might be estrangement. Help (him/her) to be
the one who stands strong in love when others create
conflicts. In Jesus' name, amen.

Week 19
CONTENTMENT

DAY
1

Be still before the LORD and wait patiently for him; do not fret when men succeed in their ways, when they carry out their wicked schemes.
—PSALM 37:7

Is the command given in this verse fair? Why or why not?

It is difficult for teens to maintain their integrity when others are trying so hard to knock it down. Many will give in to pressure in order to avoid ridicule or exclusion. Reminding them of the humiliation Christ suffered for their sake will encourage them see that those who remain true prevail in the end.

• • • • • • • • • • •

"Then I entered the shadow and everything was beautiful."
—JILL BRISCOE, FROM *GOD'S FRONT DOOR*

PRAYER: Lord, let ___ share (his/her) heart with You and seek You out when challenged. Enable (him/her) to trust in You and stand firm when necessary. In Jesus' name, amen.

109

The godly can look forward to happiness, while the wicked can expect only wrath.
—PROVERBS 11:23

What are you like when you have a happy heart? When you experience heartache?

Teens' relationships with the opposite sex can be painful. Relationships can become so centered in their lives that they grow dependant on them to influence their moods and instruct their lives. Teach them to appreciate their youth as a time of independence before they make a long-term commitment and to depend on God for their self-worth instead of on others.

• • • • • • • • • • •

"Carefulness is no sin, nor is there any grace in a solemn cast of countenance."
—JOHN NEWTON, FROM *HEROES OF THE FAITH*

PRAYER: Lord, be the Ruler over ___'s heart
as (he/she) chooses whom to date and spend
time with. Let it be those You choose, who will
build (him/her) up and not break (him/her) down,
who follow You and not the things of this world.
In Jesus' name, amen.

A man can do nothing better than to eat and drink and find satisfaction in his work. This too, I see, is from the hand of God.
—ECCLESIASTES 2:24

Does this verse mean that eating, drinking, and work are the most important things in life? If so, how can recognizing that these things come from God make them even better?

Our society values most those who are thin, with the consequence that many teens develop eating disorders. Trying to find a balance can be confusing to teens. They can easily be misled because the need to fit in often overshadows the need for good health. Provide a good example for them, and also closely observe your teen's eating habits and general health so you are aware if any issues arise.

• • • • • • • • • •

"My work, my life, must be in the spirit of a little child seeking only to know the truth and follow it."
—GEORGE WASHINGTON CARVER, FROM *HEROES OF THE FAITH*

PRAYER: Lord, reveal to ___ how to treat (his/her) body as a temple. Let (him/her) see Your perfect design in the creation of (his/her) body. Teach (him/her) how to care for (his/her) body to maintain good health. In Jesus' name, amen.

DAY 4

Each one should remain in the situation which he was in when God called him.
—1 CORINTHIANS 7:20

How does this verse help us to be more content?

Teens may consider suicide when they feel they can't endure a situation. They don't have enough experience to see how temporary the situation is. Help them to develop long-term goals and to look forward instead of backward. Encourage them to think ahead and not just look for what might relieve their problems in the here and now.

• • • • • • • • • •

"I compare the troubles which we have to undergo in the course of the year to a great bundle of fagots, far too large for us to lift. But God does not require us to carry the whole at once. He mercifully unties the bundle, and gives us first one stick, which we are to carry today, and then another, which we are to carry tomorrow, and so on."
—JOHN NEWTON, FROM *COMMEMORATION OF MARY SLESSOR*

PRAYER: Lord, show ____ Your purpose
for the situation You have chosen for (him/her)
to be in. Give (him/her) things to look forward
to and goals to meet along the way. As (he/she)
serves Your purpose, Lord, create the adult
You want (him/her) to be. In Jesus' name, amen.

DAY
5

If they obey and serve him, they will spend
the rest of their days in prosperity and
their years in contentment.
—JOB 36:11

Do you believe in God's promises given in this verse?

When teens feel hopeless, they need to stay connected to others. Find out who your teen's friends and confidantes are so you know whom to turn to when your teen won't open up to you. Sometimes teens need to vent, and they just need to hear from someone else that they are okay.

• • • • • • • • • •

How many blessings I enjoy,
That other people don't.
To weep and sigh because I'm blind,
I cannot and I won't."
—FANNY CROSBY, FROM *HEROES OF THE FAITH*

PRAYER: Lord, help ____ to see how God-controlled
(his/her) life is and to be anxious for nothing.
Show (him/her) Your hand in everything.
When (he/she) wakes and sleeps, at work
and at play, help (him/her) to know that You
are there. In Jesus' name, amen.

DAY 6

I am not saying this because I am in need, for I have learned to be content whatever the circumstances.
—PHILIPPIANS 4:11

Are you content? Or do you find yourself always wanting more?

Teens can push the limits with fashion trends. They find part of their identity in what they wear, but putting too much emphasis on style can overpower right priorities and create discontent. Teach them that if they present themselves in a respectful way they will earn the kind of positive attention that leads to true contentment.

• • • • • • • • • • •

"Do you know that if at birth I had been able to make one petition, it would have been that I should be born blind? . . . Because when I get to heaven, the first face that shall ever gladden my sight will be that of my Savior!"
—FANNY CROSBY, FROM *FANNY CROSBY THE HYMN WRITER*

PRAYER: Lord, help ___ not to be flesh-controlled in (his/her) fashion choices, and release (him/her) from the pressures to fit in. Let others see the God sense instead of the fashion sense in (him/her), and let (him/her) be proud to represent You. In Jesus' name, amen.

DAY 7

But godliness with contentment is great gain.
—1 TIMOTHY 6:6

What is gained according to this verse?

During this transitional time in their lives, help teens to learn to be content with what they have and not be disgruntled about what they don't have.

• • • • • • • • • • •

"God didn't call us to be successful, just faithful."
—MOTHER TERESA, FROM *HEROES OF THE FAITH*

PRAYER: Lord, give ___ a spirit of joy in knowing that You are what brings contentment. Let (him/her) see the qualities of meekness, patience, and kindness in You, and let (him/her) want to model those behaviors to others. In Jesus' name, amen.

Week 20
ACCEPT

DAY 1

For whoever is not against us is for us.
—MARK 9:40

How can you tell who is against you or for you?

Teens will face rejections and need to learn how to deal with them. Talking with those who make things difficult for them may help to ease the pain, but sometimes it's just too hard to shake. Since Jesus went through a lot of oppression while he was here on earth, we know he feels our pain completely.

• • • • • • • • • • •

"Be courteous to all, but intimate with few, and let those few be well tried before you give them your confidence. True friendship is a plant of slow growth, and must undergo and withstand the shocks of adversity before it is entitled to the appellation."
—GEORGE WASHINGTON, FROM *GREAT QUOTATIONS PAGE*

> PRAYER: Lord, take ___'s broken spirit and bring a calm serenity to (him/her). Soothe (his/her) broken heart and mend unseen wounds. Remind _____ that (he/she) is the apple of Your eye. In Jesus' name, amen.

DAY 2

I tell you the truth, anyone who gives you a cup of water in my name because you belong to Christ will certainly not lose his reward.
—MARK 9:41

When you help someone, do you do it in Christ's name or to get something in return?

Teens must learn tolerance for others, and not only for their own gain. Being an example for others isn't easy, especially when they are trying to fit in, but with the courage they receive from Christ to live by His example, they can find their way.

● ● ● ● ● ● ● ● ● ●

"Do all the good you can, by all the means you can, in all the ways you can, in all the places you can, at all the times you can, to all the people you can, as long as ever you can."
—JOHN WESLEY, FROM HEROES OF THE FAITH

> PRAYER: Lord, give ____ a gentle spirit to care for others as You do. Remind (him/her) of the struggles You went through and how You always did the right thing, even when others were so very wrong. Let that give (him/her) strength and fortitude to continue in Your ways. In Jesus' name, amen.

DAY 3

So I sent for you immediately, and it was good of you to come. Now we are all here in the presence of God to listen to everything the LORD has commanded you to tell us." Then Peter began to speak: "I now realize how true it is that God does not show favoritism but accepts men from every nation who fear him and do what is right. You know the message God sent to the people of Israel, telling the good news of peace through Jesus Christ, who is LORD of all."
—ACTS 10:33-36

Have you ever stereotyped what a Christian should be like?

Often in the teen world, only the most impressive are accepted. Teens may be dismayed the first time they are let down by another Christian they looked up to, especially if it is someone of stature within the church. Learning to extend grace to others when they are weak and letting go of judgmental attitudes is hard but a part of spiritual growth.

•••••••••••

"If you read history you will find that the Christians who did most for the present world were precisely those who thought most of the next. It is since Christians have largely ceased to think of the other world that they have become so ineffective in this one."
—C. S. Lewis, from *Heroes of the Faith*

PRAYER: Lord, let __ see Your way of acceptance and learn to treat others as You do. Show (him/her) Your mercy, Lord. Teach (him/her) about the ultimate unconditional love that only You can truly give and that we must try to live by. In Jesus' name, amen.

DAY
4

While Peter was still speaking these words, the Holy Spirit came on all who heard the message.
—ACTS 10:44

Do you ever feel the presence of the Holy Spirit?

Teens don't always ask for help when they need it. They may not know who to trust. Friends can come and go, but one who walks in the path of the Holy Spirit should be kept and valued.

•••••••••••

He ate and drank the precious words,
His spirit grew robust;
He knew no more that he was poor,

Nor that his frame was dust.
He danced along the dingy days,
And this bequest of wings
Was but a book—what liberty
A loosened spirit brings!
—EMILY DICKINSON, FROM *AMERICAN POEMS*

PRAYER: Lord, encourage ___ to bring (his/her) broken spirit to You. When all others fail (him/her), let _____ always know that (he/she) can come to You, the only one who offers unfailing forgiveness and love. In Jesus' name, amen.

DAY 5

"So if God gave them the same gift as he gave us, who believed in the LORD *Jesus Christ, who was I to think that I could oppose God?" Whey they heard this, they had no further objections and praised God, saying, "So then, God has granted even the Gentiles repentance unto life."*
—ACTS 11:17

When you look around at people you associate with, are there some you would like to withhold repentance from? How do you treat those people?

Teens, like adults, can get caught up in judging others. It comes so easily to all of us, and it is difficult to stop. If we can remind our teens of times when they were judged unfairly, they may look at others differently and realize they need that same grace.

• • • • • • • • • •

"Christian love, either towards God or towards man,
is an affair of the will."
—C. S. LEWIS, FROM *MERE CHRISTIANITY*

PRAYER: Lord, protect ___ from others' passing judgment on (him/her) or abusing (his/her) friendship. Let (him/her) feel Your acceptance and offer that same acceptance to others.
In Jesus' name, amen.

For all of you who were baptized into Christ have clothed yourselves with Christ.
—GALATIANS 3:27

What does it look like to be clothed in Christ?

Teens will undergo many transformations during adolescence. We hope these transformations include that of godly purpose. Help to foster this by encouraging them to find a small group and a mentor to lean on.

• • • • • • • • • • •

"Be faithful in little practices of love, of little sacrifices . . . which will build in you the life of holiness—make you Christ-like."
—MOTHER TERESA, FROM HER PRIVATE WRITINGS

PRAYER: Lord, wash ___ with Your purifying, living water. Keep (him/her) clothed in You, surrounded by You. Let (him/her) feel Your closeness all around (him/her) and Your protection, warmth, and comfort. In Jesus' name, amen.

There is neither Jew nor Greek, slave nor free, male nor female, for you are all one in Christ Jesus.
—GALATIANS 3:28

We tend to separate people into categories. Is it hard for you to see people that way if they are Christians?

Teaching acceptance of others' race, creed, and color seems like a given, but are we being more tolerant than accepting? We need to learn to accept those God has created in the same way He does and not just grudgingly tolerate them.

• • • • • • • • • •

"I have a dream that my four little children will one day live in a nation where they will not be judged by the color of their skin but by the content of their character."
—MARTIN LUTHER KING, JR, FROM *GREAT QUOTES FROM GREAT LEADERS*

PRAYER: Lord, shield ___ from those who make evil plans against You, and teach (him/her) to seek those who serve You. Teach us to accept those of good will no matter what their color or nationality is. In Jesus' name, amen.

Week 21
RESPECT

DAY
1

*"Honor your father and your mother,
so that you may live long in the land
the Lord your God is giving you."*
—EXODUS 20:12

Do you feel that your teen honors you?

Teens need to accept more responsibilities as they grow older. One of these is to continue to honor their parents. Even when they are independent adults, they don't have permission to be any less respectful to their parents.

• • • • • • • • • •

*"Definiteness of purpose is the starting point
of all achievement."*
—CLEMENT STONE, FROM *WISE WORDS AND QUOTES*

PRAYER: Lord, turn ___ away from selfishness
and neglect and toward bonds of commitment.
Let (him/her) see how much we parents care
for (him/her), and help ___ to always see us
as a refuge and support. In Jesus' name, amen.

Listen, my sons, to a father's instruction;
pay attention and gain understanding.
—PROVERBS 4:1

When you look back on your life, does this verse seem like good advice? Why?

It is a teen's nature to rebel, to assert independence and not heed much-needed advice, but for a parent to just be there can sometimes be enough to help them to make right choices. We can pray that they respond as they should and not as they might be tempted to.

• • • • • • • • • • •

"The art of being wise is the art of knowing what to overlook."
—WILLIAM JAMES, FROM *THINKEXIST QUOTES*

> PRAYER: Lord, let ___ see the legacy in (his/her)
> grasp so that (he/she) will someday be able
> to establish a godly home. Teach us how to be
> good parents and to be the kind of example that
> we should be even when it is hard and the results
> are questionable. Help us to parent through
> Your wisdom. In Jesus' name, amen.

My son, keep your father's commands and
do not forsake your mother's teaching.
—PROVERBS 6:20

If you have followed the advice in this verse, did it work out better or worse for you and others involved?

Teens tend to want to be left alone and not be as involved in family time as when they were younger. But keeping family time sacred is as important for them as it is for you. Although teens might participate grudgingly, the time is never wasted, and they may actually remember those experiences fondly when they are older.

• • • • • • • • • • •

"When I was a tiny child I turned from the window
out of which I was watching a snowstorm, and hopefully asked,
'Momma, do we believe in winter?' "
—FROM *PORTNOY'S COMPLAINT* BY PHILIP ROTH

PRAYER: Lord, help ___ to eliminate (his/her)
independent attitude just for a moment and make
time for family. Let the interaction between all of us
be sweet and productive, and let the memories of
good times spent together linger through to (his/her)
adulthood. In Jesus' name, amen.

| DAY
4 | *Train a child in the way he should go,*
and when he is old he will not turn from it.
—PROVERBS 22:6 |

What happens between childhood and being old?

Teens are in the middle of a long life journey that will be full of loss and gain, good times and bad. There will be valleys to endure and mountains for them to climb. Doing what we can to encourage them through the difficult experiences and help them to flourish when they go through happy times will enable them to persist and learn important life lessons along the way.

• • • • • • • • • • •

"Be not angry that you cannot make others as you wish them to
be, since you cannot make yourself as you wish to be."
—THOMAS À KEMPIS, FROM *IMITATION OF CHRIST*

PRAYER: Lord, help ___ not to waiver in following
You throughout (his/her) life. When there are troubles, Lord, remind (him/her) to come to You, and
when times are good remind (him/her) to praise You
and give You glory. In Jesus' name, amen.

DAY 5

And he took the children in his arms,
put his hands on them and blessed them.
—MARK 10:16

How do you imagine you would feel if you were hugged by Jesus and he blessed you?

For a teen to feel that all his or her mistakes have been erased will create a great renewal. Even to imagine it can be heart-moving. We need to encourage our teens to think about how they should live out their lives until that day when they are with Christ again.

• • • • • • • • • • •

"Family bonds are formed less by moments of celebration and of crisis than by the quiet, undramatic accretion of minutiae—the remark on the way out the door, the chore undone, the unexpected smile."
—GEORGE HOWE COLT, FROM *LIFE* MAGAZINE ARTICLE

PRAYER: Lord, lay Your merciful hand on and bless ___ as (he/she) starts anew. Let (him/her) sit at Your feet and confess all (his/her) transgressions, worries, hopes, and dreams. In Jesus' name, amen.

DAY 6

Fathers, do not exasperate your children;
instead, bring them up in the training and
instruction of the Lord.
—EPHESIANS 6:4

If you feel that your father exasperated you when you were a child, how might you avoid exasperating your teen?

Teens may feel out of control because of a bad day or because of the ever-changing chemicals flowing throughout their bodies. Hormones are powerful and can cause them to become easily exasperated. Parents can help by remaining patient, looking for patterns in their behavior, and knowing what questions to ask.

• • • • • • • • • •

"Forget goals. Value the process."
—JIM BOUTON FROM *MEDITATIONS FOR PARENTS WHO DO TOO MUCH*

PRAYER: Lord, release ___ from negative emotions and use us as an instrument of restoration, and not to exasperate. Help us to understand our teen and know when to push and when to just support (him/her). In Jesus' name, amen.

DAY
7

Don't let anyone look down on you because you are young, but set an example for the believers in speech, in life, in love, in faith and in purity.
—1 TIMOTHY 4:12

If someone is getting you down, where can you find the strength to set a good example?

When teens feel bullied or mistreated, they need to find strength to stand firm. Your encouragement and advice can work wonders if delivered in love, so preparing for dialog ahead of time will help. These situations often build up, so the quicker the situation is defused, the better.

• • • • • • • • • •

"The thing to do is to supply light and not heat."
—WOODROW WILSON, FROM *GREAT QUOTES FROM GREAT LEADERS*

PRAYER: Lord, deliver ___ from emotions that may cause self-doubt, and free (him/her) from harassment. In Jesus' name, amen.

Week 22

CHOSEN

The LORD gave this command to Joshua son of Nun: "Be strong and courageous, for you will bring the Israelites into the land I promised them on oath, and I myself will be with you."
—DEUTERONOMY 31:23

How do you think you would recognize a call from God?

The attitudes teens give us can be very frustrating. Remembering that God is guiding you, that your teen's heart is good, and that he or she may simply need encouragement to behave the way they should can help you to be patient and not get discouraged.

• • • • • • • • • • •

"People may doubt what you say, but they believe what you do."
—ANONYMOUS

PRAYER: Lord, help ___ not to take (his/her) eyes off You and to trust You in all circumstances. Teach (him/her) this night and day, when awake or asleep. In Jesus' name, amen.

DAY 2

When the angel of the LORD appeared to Gideon, he said, "The LORD is with you, mighty warrior."
—JUDGES 6:12

What can you expect from God if you answer His call?

No matter what the past may be, teens can always make a new start with God. Encourage them to be ready to do His will with all their hearts and souls when He calls, and God will be with them.

• • • • • • • • • •

"How does the Meadow flower its bloom unfold?
Because the lovely little flower is free down to its root,
and in that freedom bold."
—WILLIAM WORDSWORTH

PRAYER: Lord, set ____ free of the past and give (him/her) the needed strength for the future. Help (him/her) to know the plans You have made for (him/her) and how to live out those plans to glorify You. In Jesus' name, amen.

DAY 3

He sent Moses his servant, and Aaron, whom he had chosen.
—PSALM 105:26

How do you respond to others who have been chosen by God?

At times teens feel like underachievers, especially when they encounter so much competition. Helping them find their uniqueness and their strengths can help them to set themselves apart and grow in their individual talents.

• • • • • • • • • •

Enough, if something from our hands have power
To live, and act, and serve the future hour.
—WILLIAM WORDSWORTH, FROM "AFTERTHOUGHT"

PRAYER: Lord, give me the words to say to ___ when (he/she) feels less than others. Help me build (him/her) up to realize (his/her) potential. Grow ___ to be what You will (him/her) to be.
In Jesus' name, amen.

DAY 4

"Come, follow me," Jesus said,
"and I will make you fishers of men."
—MATTHEW 4:19

Does Jesus' call apply to you? If it does, who do you think you need to fish for?

Some teens may feel inhibited about talking with others about their faith. Knowing scripture and having a testimony to share will help to give them the confidence they need.

• • • • • • • • • •

"A good question for an atheist is to serve him a fine dinner,
and then ask if he believes there is a cook."
—THE ANGLICAN DIGEST

PRAYER: Lord, anoint ___ with Your Spirit and show (him/her) how to share Jesus with others. Give (him/her) the ability to remember Your Word and to offer Your gospel to all with a gentle heart.
In Jesus' name, amen.

DAY 5

As he walked along, he saw Levi son of Alphaeus sitting at the tax collector's booth. "Follow me," Jesus told him, and Levi got up and followed him.
—MARK 2:14

What do you think you would be reluctant to give up if you were called by Jesus?

Teens easily get caught up in the power of money. We need to set an example for them by placing importance on our faith and not on the material things of this world.

• • • • • • • • • •

"God does not give us overcoming life: He gives life as we overcome. The strain is the strength. If there is no strain, there is no strength. Are you asking God to give you life and liberty and joy? He cannot, unless you will accept the strain. Immediately you face the strain, you will get the strength."
—OSWALD CHAMBERS, FROM *MY UTMOST FOR HIS HIGHEST*

PRAYER: Lord, keep ___ from becoming entangled in the trap of evil that money can become. Let (him/her) rise above the pleasures material things seem to promise and know that You have chosen (him/her) for Your service. In Jesus' name, amen.

DAY
6

You did not choose me, but I choose you and appointed you to go and bear fruit—fruit that will last. Then the Father will give you whatever you ask in my name.
—JOHN 15:16

If this verse is true, what is it that makes us hesitate to accept God's call?

Teens pull away from their family as they mature. Although we should try to steer them in the right direction, ultimately the choice is theirs as to how they live their lives. Instead of judging, we need to remind them that God calls them to live for Him.

• • • • • • • • • •

"We are called to be salt to others. So give them salt! It will lead them to drink."
—ANONYMOUS

PRAYER: Lord, reveal to ___ those who bear good fruit, and preserve those friendships. And if (he/she) goes astray, help (him/her) find the way back to You through Your loving direction and correction.
In Jesus' name, amen.

DAY 7

No one takes this honor upon himself;
he must be called by God, just as Aaron was.
—HEBREWS 5:4

Why would a person fake a calling from God? How do you feel about a person who would do this?

Teens often have trouble knowing what their call is, let alone what others' are. Learning to discern through God's eyes will keep them from being drawn into error by others' bad example.

• • • • • • • • • • •

"I didn't bother to consult God on this decision.
I knew beyond any doubt that he would agree with me.
But this was one time when God did not honor my wishes.
He had other plans. And I am so thankful He did."
—THE SOUP MAN, AKA DAVID TIMOTHY, FROM *IS GOD ON VACATION?*

Prayer: Lord, defend ___ from those who lead false lives, and purify (him/her) in Your refining fire. Help (him/her) to see when people aren't who they appear to be, and guard ___'s heart. In Jesus' name, amen.

Week 23

HOPE

DAY 1

Be strong and take heart, all you who hope in the LORD.
—PSALM 31:24

What gives you heart and makes you strong?

Although your teen may feel that rules cramp their style, setting boundaries actually gives teens the chance to show their maturity and gain the independence they seek. By granting privileges to reward good behavior, parents can encourage negative behaviors to fade away.

• • • • • • • • • • •

"Not until I went into the churches of America and heard her pulpits aflame with righteousness did I understand the secret of her genius and power. America is great because America is good, and if America ever ceases to be good, America will cease to be great."
—ALEXIS DE TOCQUEVILLE, FROM *PATCHES OF GODLIGHT*

PRAYER: Lord, let ___ see the good that comes from discipline and that it is done out of love. Let (him/her) make good choices and be wise in what (he/she) does with the leeway given to (him/her). Surround ___ with Your guardian angels, and keep (him/her) safe. In Jesus' name, amen.

133

DAY
2

*But now, L*ORD*, what do I look for?*
My hope is in you.
—PSALM 39:7

When you feel hopeless, do you turn to the Lord? How does that help?

Teens may not know the difference between stress and depression and may need help figuring out the difference. Many things can cause teens to feel forlorn or sad, but that doesn't necessarily mean that they are depressed. Learning their cycles and hormone changes can be key for them in learning to have hope.

• • • • • • • • • • •

"Courage is not having the strength to go on;
it is going on when you don't have the strength.
Industry and determination can do anything that genius and
advantage can do and many things that they cannot."
—THEODORE ROOSEVELT, FROM *WISDOM QUOTES*

PRAYER: Lord, keep the Evil One's deceptive thoughts from ___ , and don't let (him/her) feel shamed by Satan's manipulations. Help (him/her) to understand (his/her) body and mind so (he/she) can know what will pass in time and what (he/she) needs help with. In Jesus' name, amen.

DAY
3

Now faith is being sure of what we hope for
and certain of what we do not see.
—HEBREWS 11:1

Have you ever had faith in someone who ended up failing you? Compare this experience with your faith in Jesus.

Gossip is the ruin of many a teen relationship, and learning to trust again when one has been wounded is difficult. Learning how much personal information to share and who is safe to share it with can help teens avoid a bad experience.

● ● ● ● ● ● ● ● ● ●

*"One ought never to turn one's back on a threatened danger
and try to run away from it. If you do that, you will double
the danger. But if you meet it promptly and
without flinching, you will reduce the danger by half."*
—WINSTON CHURCHILL, FROM *QUOTATIONS PAGE*

PRAYER: Lord, deliver ____ from (his/her) enemies.
Let them be revealed and driven backward,
away from (him/her). Help ____ to lean on You
for understanding and healing from others' wrongful
deeds. Let (him/her) see clearly who is friend and
who is foe. In Jesus' name, amen.

DAY 4

*Not only so, but we also rejoice in our sufferings,
because we know that suffering produces perseverance,
perseverance, character; and character, hope.
And hope does not disappoint us, because God has
poured out his love into our hearts by the Holy Spirit,
whom he has given us.*
—ROMANS 5:35

**As you look back, how has this verse been true for you? If you
are suffering now, does this promise give you hope?**

If teens did not go through hard times, they would grow to be
selfish, immature, stale adults. We all know people who carry
these traits. We need to remember them when our teen is struggling and have confidence that their struggles will result in perseverance, character, and the hope that does not disappoint.

● ● ● ● ● ● ● ● ● ●

*"I remember the story of the old man who said
on his deathbed that he had had a lot of trouble in his life,
most of which never happened."*
—WINSTON CHURCHILL, FROM *PATCHES OF GODLIGHT*

For in this hope we were saved. But hope that is seen is no hope at all. Who hopes for what he already has?
—ROMANS 8:24

What are you hoping for? Will it require faith or work for you to gain it? If it requires work on your part, is it faith?

Teens go through many changes and may lose some hopes and dreams along the way. Believing that God has a plan and is directing them in that plan requires unconditional faith.

• • • • • • • • • • •

"Understanding is the reward of faith. Therefore seek not to understand that you may believe, but believe that you may understand."
—ST. AUGUSTINE, FROM *CROSSINGS*

PRAYER: Lord, help ___ to never lean on (his/her) own understanding but to hope in You at all times. Keep (him/her) untarnished by the world and let (him/her) see (himself/herself) as You do. In Jesus' name, amen.

Be joyful in hope, patient in affliction, faithful in prayer.
—ROMANS 12:12

Can you think of anything that would be better advice in suffering than this verse?

Teens tend to see everything as being all about "me." During times of affliction this attitude may cause them to turn inward for self-protection. Teach your teen that reaching out to others during these times actually helps them to heal and can give them hope.

• • • • • • • • • • •

"Prayer is either a sheer illusion or a personal contact between . . . incomplete persons (ourselves) and the utterly concrete Person.

*Prayer in the sense of petition, asking for things, is a small part
of it; confession and penitence are its threshold, adoration its
sanctuary, the presence and vision and enjoyment of God its bread
and wine. In it God shows Himself to us. That He answers prayer
is a corollary—not necessarily the most important one—
from that revelation. What He does is learned from what He is."*
—C. S. LEWIS, FROM *THE ESSENTIAL C. S. LEWIS*

PRAYER: Lord, give ____ a heart that is quick to heal
from the pain caused by Your cleansing from all
unrighteousness. Show (him/her) the goodness of
Your ways and the comfort and hope to be found in
You. In Jesus' name, amen.

*Everyone who has this hope in him
purifies himself, just as he is pure.*
—1 JOHN 3:3

When have you felt pure because of your faith and not because of something you did?

Teens want to be liked and are tempted to do things to win
acceptance. This may lead to impure acts and thoughts.
Knowing they are forgiven by God even before a sin is committed will assure them of His love and nurture a deep desire to live
for Him.

• • • • • • • • • • •

"The lowest ebb is the turn of the tide."
—HENRY W. LONGFELLOW, FROM *THE OTHER PAGES*

PRAYER: Lord, help ____ not to waver under the
pressures of the world, but to stand strong in You
and carry Your Word in (his/her) heart and on
(his/her) tongue. In Jesus' name, amen.

Week 24

LIGHT

DAY
1

God saw that the light was good, and he separated the light from the darkness.
—GENESIS 1:4

Which do you like better, light or darkness? Why?

Sometimes it is hard for a teen to know the difference between spiritual darkness and light. People, activities, books, and movies can all seem harmless when "everyone" approves of them. Learning to call on the Holy Spirit will help them to choose what is right.

• • • • • • • • • •

"It is really a bad world . . . an incredibly bad world. Yet in the midst of it, I have found a quiet and holy people. They have discovered a joy, which is a thousand times better than any pleasure of this sinful life. They are despised and persecuted, but they care not. They have overcome the world. These people . . . are the Christians . . . and I am one of them."
—CYPRIAN, FROM *PATCHES OF GODLIGHT*

PRAYER: Lord, keep ___ strong when (he/she) is weak. Break down the powers of evil and take charge of (his/her) spirit. Help ___ to grow confident in (his/her) choices in spite of the pressure of others.
In Jesus' name, amen.

139

DAY 2

The LORD is my light and my salvation—whom shall I fear? The LORD is the stronghold of my life—of whom shall I be afraid?
—PSALM 27:1

What does it mean to you to say, "The Lord is my light"?

The way to the light is not always clear to a teen. Many distortions can lead teens off the path into darkness before they even realize they have fallen. Following God's will can appear too difficult at times, but we know it will always lead to the light.

• • • • • • • • • • •

"The fear of the Lord is the beginning of wisdom."
—PROVERBS 9:10

PRAYER: Lord, I pray that ___ will live a clean life in a dark world. Make (him/her) shine like a beacon of light and become salt of the earth. Let others see that light and want to hear (his/her) words, which come from You. In Jesus' name, amen.

DAY 3

Your sun will never set again, and your moon will wane no more; the LORD will be your everlasting light, and your days of sorrow will end.
—ISAIAH 60:20

How does this verse encourage you?

What joy it is for teens to know that the Lord will never let darkness overcome them. If they understand this, they will become strong in everything they do and say and will be able to stand firm for Him.

• • • • • • • • • • •

"Love must be as much a light, as it is a flame."
—HENRY D. THOREAU, FROM *PATCHES OF GODLIGHT*

PRAYER: Lord, fulfill Your purposes for ___. Do not abandon your work in (him/her). Help (him/her) to use the gifts you have given according to Your will to further Your kingdom. In Jesus' name, amen.

*"You are the light of the world.
A city on a hill cannot be hidden."*
—MATTHEW 5:14

If you are the light of your world, who benefits?

What an incredible position to be in, to be a light for God. Teens can do amazing things if they conduct themselves in ways worthy of respect and become persons to whom others look for wisdom and understanding.

• • • • • • • • • •

"Nobody worries about Christ as long as he can be kept shut up in churches. He is quite safe there. But there is always trouble if you try to let him out."
—GEOFFREY STUDDERT-KENNEDY, FROM *THE COLLECTED POETRY OF G. A. STUDDERT-KENNEDY*

PRAYER: Lord, let ___ turn from the darkness to Your light, away from Satan to You. Mold (his/her) behavior so others will look at (him/her) as one with great integrity. In Jesus' name, amen.

*The light shines in the darkness,
but the darkness has not understood it.*
—JOHN 1:5

When have you shined your light and it just didn't seem to make any difference to those around you?

Encourage your teen to stay active in doing God's good work. It is important for teens to have others they can turn to for support and ideas to keep their focus on Him.

• • • • • • • • • • •

"Character is what you are in the dark."
—DWIGHT L. MOODY, FROM *HEROES OF THE FAITH*

PRAYER: Lord, help ___ not to be ashamed of (his/her) faith in You. Give (him/her) the words needed to stand up for what (he/she) believes. When ___ is weary, call (him/her) to rest in You and let You help carry (his/her) burdens. In Jesus' name, amen.

DAY
6

When Jesus spoke again to the people, he said, "I am the light of the world. Whoever follows me will never walk in darkness, but will have the light of life."
—JOHN 8:12

What kind of light does Jesus give you for your walk with Him?

Teens are not always clear about what their spiritual gift is. Listening to the positive things others say about them can help them to learn what their calling may be and provide guidance in their walk with the Lord.

• • • • • • • • • • •

They say best men are molded out of faults.
—FROM *MEASURE FOR MEASURE* BY WILLIAM SHAKESPEARE

PRAYER: Lord, let ___ walk with You in devotion and faithfulness, doing good even when others don't. Help (him/her) learn what to do with the gift You have given (him/her) and shine Your light on (his/her) path. In Jesus' name, amen.

142

*This is the message we have heard from him
and declare to you: God is light, in him there
is no darkness at all.*
—1 JOHN 1:5

**If it is true that God is light and there is no darkness in Him,
how do you explain times when you are confused?**

The assurance that there is no darkness in God can be a great comfort to teens. We as humans are so far from God's absolute light that we can never completely comprehend it. We may have difficulty understanding how a righteous God can allow bad things to happen, but we can have confidence that all power belongs to Him and that He is just.

• • • • • • • • • • •

*May I bring union in place of discord;
Truth, replacing error;
Faith, where once there was doubt;
Hope, for despair;
Light, where there was darkness;
"Joy to replace sadness."*
—PRAYER OF FRANCIS OF ASSISI, FROM *POETIC EXPRESSIONS*

PRAYER: Lord, help ___ not to grow tired of doing good. Give (him/her) the strength to remain faithful through the hard times and reap a harvest in Your name. Remind (him/her) of the outcome, the reward You have waiting for (him/her).
In Jesus' name, amen.

Week 25
GLORY

Ascribe to the LORD the glory due his name.
Bring an offering and come before him;
worship the LORD in the splendor of his holiness.
—1 CHRONICLES 16:29

Is it easier for you to give God glory or to give Him an offering?

Teens often depend on material things to make them joyful, but God provides joy apart from things. It is interesting to hear what offerings teens would consider giving to God. What a person feels is worthy of an offering can tell you a lot about that person.

• • • • • • • • • •

"It is important to learn respect, and obedience to the 'inner must' of godliness is to be a state of soul with me."
—JIM ELLIOT, FROM *HEROES OF THE FAITH*

PRAYER: Lord, I pray that ___ will give to You (his/her) most precious offerings and that (he/she) will honor You as You deserve to be honored. Let the offering be sweet to Your eyes and pleasing to Your ears as You are glorified. In Jesus' name, amen.

DAY 2

I will praise you, O LORD my God, with all my heart; I will glorify your name forever.
—PSALM 86:12

How do you praise God? How do you glorify His name?

Teens often look to what they do for joy, not to the Lord for what He does. This is the humanity in us that causes selfishness and is our downfall. If our eyes are always looking up to Him, the focus will remain off our own desires and on the Father.

● ● ● ● ● ● ● ● ● ●

"The greatest works are done by the ones.
The hundreds do not often do much,
the companies never; it is the units,
the single individuals, that are the power and the might."
—CHARLES H. SPURGEON, FROM *HEROES OF THE FAITH*

PRAYER: Lord, let ___ be proud to bear Your name and let (him/her) bring joy to hungry souls because of You. Help ___ not to let others bring (him/her) down, but let them see the light You have put inside (his/her) soul. In Jesus' name, amen.

DAY 3

I will praise God's name in song and glorify him with thanksgiving.
—PSALM 69:30

This verse tells how David worshiped. When you sing songs about God, do you think of it as glorifying Him? Will you start?

Teens love music, and today's Christian songs run the spectrum of genres, which leaves a good chance that teens can find some form that suits them. Putting positive lyrics into their heads can help them keep their minds on Christ.

• • • • • • • • • •

*"A true love to God must begin with a delight
in His holiness, and not with a delight
in any other attribute; for no other attribute
is truly lovely without this."*
—JONATHAN EDWARDS, FROM *TREATISE CONCERNING RELIGIOUS AFFECTIONS*

PRAYER: Lord, keep ___ close to You. Everywhere
Your hand will guide (him/her) and hold (him/her)
fast by Your Spirit. Let ___ rejoice in You
by singing Your praises. In Jesus' name, amen.

DAY
4

*You are my God, and I will give you thanks;
you are my God, and I will exalt you.*
—PSALM 118:28

What do you give God credit for?

To look at the good God has provided us gives such encouragement. For teens to think about all He has done for them puts a new perspective on turning to Him and giving thanks.

• • • • • • • • • •

*"Christian perfection is the loving of God
with all our heart, and our neighbour as ourselves."*
—JOHN WESLEY, FROM *PLAIN ACCOUNT OF CHRISTIAN PERFECTION*

PRAYER: Lord, let ___ lift (his/her) hands and claim
You as (his/her) God. Remind (him/her) to give
You thanks for all You have done and will do.
In Jesus' name, amen.

147

*The people were amazed when they saw
the mute speaking, the crippled made well,
the lame walking, and the blind seeing.
And they praised the God of Israel.*
—MATTHEW 15:31

Whom would you praise for the kinds of healings mentioned in this verse? God or the doctor or both?

We need to learn to be responsible in all things, both earthly and spiritual. To whom and what to give credit on this earth can be difficult to perceive at times. But it is always appropriate to give thanks to God for His mighty works of healing.

• • • • • • • • • •

*Thou art coming to a King,
Large petitions with thee bring;
For His grace and power are such,
None can ever ask too much.*
—JOHN NEWTON, FROM "COME, MY SOUL, THY SUIT PREPARE"

PRAYER: Lord, reach down with Your mighty hand
and deliver ___ from the evils of this world.
Help (him/her) to give credit to You for all You do.
Help (him/her) to always remember You are
the One who gives gifts, and You can also
take them away. In Jesus' name, amen.

*"You are worthy, our LORD and God, to receive glory
and honor and power, for you created all things, and
by your will they were created and have their being."*
—REVELATION 4:11

What does this verse mean when it says that God is worthy?

To think of all that God has created by the touch of His hand is overwhelming. Teens often like to debate things they took for granted as children. These are good opportunities to get them to think about what the truth really is and where they stand.

• • • • • • • • • • •

"I love to think of nature as an unlimited broadcasting station, through which God speaks to us every hour, if we will only tune in."
—GEORGE WASHINGTON CARVER, FROM *HEROES OF THE FAITH*

PRAYER: Lord, let ___ call upon You, knowing You will answer and tell (him/her) great things. Remind (him/her) that You embody all wisdom and knowledge, that no one knows (his/her) own heart and mind as You do. In Jesus' name, amen.

Who will not fear you, O LORD, and bring glory to your name? For you alone are holy. All nations will come and worship before you, for your righteous acts have been revealed.
—REVELATION 15:4

How and when do you think the nations will come and worship before God? Do you have faith that this is going to happen?

Something beautiful and peaceful happens when we meditate on God's glory. That people from all nations will one day fall down in worship before Him is amazing. When your teen feels alone in his or her faith, a reminder that one day every knee will bow before our God can give him or her the assurance to remain faithful.

• • • • • • • • • • •

"In commanding us to glorify him, God is inviting us to enjoy him."
—C. S. LEWIS, FROM *HEROES OF THE FAITH*

PRAYER: Lord, let ____ see (himself/herself)
as one of Your beloved sons or daughters.
Give (him/her) a heart to fear and love You.
Gather (him/her) into Your flock and claim
(him/her) as Your own. In Jesus' name, amen.

Week 26
AUTHORITY

| DAY
1 | *Do not revile the king even in your thoughts,*
or curse the rich in your bedroom,
because a bird of the air may carry
your words, and a bird on the wing
may report what you say.
—ECCLESIASTES 10:20 |

Do you ever revile those in authority?

The example we set for our teens speaks louder than our words. If we don't treat those in authority over us with respect, how can we expect our teens to be respectful of others? So often in the teen world defiance of authority is thought of as cool, and disrespectful bahavior is almost taken for granted, not only by their peers, but also by teachers and other authority figures. Acting this way can damage a teen's reputation beyond calculation. Our words and actions are the best way to teach our teens to curb the urge to disrespect.

• • • • • • • • • • •

The disappearance of a sense of responsibility
is the most far-reaching consequence
of submission to authority.
—STANLEY MILGRAM, FROM *WISDOM QUOTES*

> PRAYER: Lord, I pray that ___ will have a spirit of respect and courtesy, that (he/she) will be honorable and known as someone who is mature in their ways. Keep (him/her) from being swayed, and help (him/her) to stand strong when tempted to follow the crowd. In Jesus' name, amen.

DAY 2

Also, seek the peace and prosperity of the city to which I have carried you into exile. Pray to the LORD for it, because if it prospers, you too will prosper.
—JEREMIAH 29:7

Do you regularly pray for the peace and prosperity of your nation and city?

God commands us to respect the legitimate authority He has placed over us. When those in authority are not wise or just, that may be difficult for both adults and teens to do. At such times remind your teen that he or she is a citizen of heaven and that God's wisdom and justice will ultimately prevail in this world as it does in heaven.

• • • • • • • • • • •

"We are not citizens of this world, trying to make our way to Heaven; we are citizens of Heaven trying to make our way through this world. That radical Christian insight can be life-changing. We are not to live so as to earn God's love, inherit Heaven, and purchase our salvation. All those are given to us as gifts; gifts bought by Jesus on the cross and handed over to us. We are to live as God's redeemed, as heirs of Heaven, and as citizens of another land: the Kingdom of God. . . . We live as those who are on a journey home; a home we know will have the lights on and the door open and our Father waiting for us when we arrive. That means in all adversity our worship of God is joyful, our life is hopeful, our future is secure. There is nothing we can lose on earth that can rob us of the treasures God has given us and will give us."
—THE LANDISFARNE, FROM THE *ANGELICAN DIGEST*

PRAYER: Lord, let ___ see what Your purpose is
for (him/her). Give (him/her) the willingness
to submit and an attitude of love for those
in authority over (him/her). During the times
when we feel as if we are in exile, remind us
that You will bring justice for those who
are oppressed. Help us to remain patient
while we wait on You. In Jesus' name, amen.

DAY 3

*Paul replied, "Brothers, I did not realize
that he was the high priest; for it is written,
'Do not speak evil about the ruler of your people.' "*
—ACTS 23:5

How do you speak about those who have authority over you?

When we are able to vote, we feel we have some control over who will lead our government. But God has a hand in the decision. We are called to support our leaders on every level with prayer and our respect. Remember that teens listen to what we say about those in authority and act likewise.

• • • • • • • • • • •

*"We do not need to get good laws to restrain bad people.
We need to get good people to restrain bad laws."*
—G. K. CHESTERTON, FROM *PATCHES OF GODLIGHT*

PRAYER: Lord, help ___ to strive to show respect
for those in authority over (him/her).
Let (him/her) look to You for wisdom when
(he/she) is old enough to make decisions
about those who will rule over our country.
In Jesus' name, amen.

Everyone must submit himself to the governing authorities, for there is no authority except that which God has established. The authorities that exist have been established by God. Consequently, he who rebels against the authority is rebelling against what God has instituted, and those who do so will bring judgment on themselves.
—ROMANS 13:12

Do you believe this goes for bad authorities too? How can you submit to bad authority?

In trying to gain their independence, teens may start to rebel against authority. Even when they disagree with you, their teachers, or others in authority, they need to keep their attitudes in check so as not to become disrespectful.

• • • • • • • • • •

"The true test of civilization is, not the census, nor the size of the cities, nor the crops, but the kind of man that the country turns out."
—RALPH W. EMERSON, FROM *PATCHES OF GODLIGHT*

PRAYER: Lord, give ____ the spirit of submission, choosing to yield when You call (him/her) to do so. Help (him/her) learn to lean on Your understanding and not on (his/her) own. In Jesus' name, amen.

I urge, then, first of all, that requests, prayers, intercession and thanksgiving be made for everyone.
—1 TIMOTHY 2:1

Are there people you would like to leave out of your requests, prayers, intercessions, and thanksgiving? Do you?

Teens need to know that being truly saved means a change in their life. It isn't easy for any of us to pray and ask for good things for those we don't have good feelings toward, but we know it's what Christ would do and need to follow suit. Modeling this attitude for teens has more of an effect that anything we say.

•••••••••••

*"Never has the world had a greater need for love
than in our day. People are hungry for love. We don't have
time to stop and smile at each other. We are all in such a hurry.
Pray. Ask for the necessary grace. Pray to be able to understand
how much Jesus loved us, so that you can love others."*
—MOTHER TERESA, FROM *HEROES OF THE FAITH*

PRAYER: Lord, give ____ a spirit of gratitude and a willingness to pray for everyone, even those who may have wronged (him/her). In Jesus' name, amen.

DAY 6

*Submit yourselves for the LORD's sake to every
authority instituted among men; whether to the king,
as the supreme authority, or to governors, who are
sent by him to punish those who do wrong and
to commend those who do right.*
—1 PETER 2:13-14

According to these scriptures, what reason do we have to rebel or disobey?

It's easy to think that we are justified in rebelling against bad leaders, but if God has instituted every authority among men, then we owe even them the respect due their position. Teens may not always agree with our decisions, but although they need to have the freedom to express their feelings, it should always be done respectfully.

•••••••••••

*"For us, with the rule of right and wrong given us by Christ, there
is nothing for which we have no standard."*
—FROM *WAR AND PEACE* BY LEO TOLSTOY

PRAYER: Lord, help ___ to see that through submitting to authority (he/she) is being loyal to You. Give (him/her) a zeal for fidelity to Your ways. Remind (him/her) of how humble Jesus was when taken before authorities and help (him/her) to live by that example. In Jesus' name, amen.

DAY
7

Show proper respect to everyone: Love the brotherhood of believers, fear God, honor the king.
—I PETER 2:17

Do you think you should show respect to everyone in all situations? Why or why not?

Sometimes shame blinds us to our own responsibility for things that happen to us. When teens are not honoring you it is important for you to help them see things clearly. Once they realize how their actions affect you as their parents, they will hopefully seek more acceptable ways of communicating.

• • • • • • • • • • •

"The only thing necessary for the triumph of evil is for good men to do nothing."
—EDMUND BURKE, FROM *PATCHES OF GODLIGHT*

PRAYER: Lord, show ___ the fruitfulness of humility, and give (him/her) a willingness to submit to authority. Let others see this as strong and not weak, admirable and not unworthy, and want to know You because of _____'s actions. In Jesus' name, amen.

Week 27

BROKENNESS

DAY 1

The sacrifices of God are a broken spirit;
a broken and contrite heart, O God,
you will not despise.
—PSALMS 51:17

What does it mean to you to have a broken spirit in God's eyes?

When we sin, God allows us to become broken, and then picks up the pieces and makes us whole again. Teens often fall into the trap of expecting independence without responsibility, which can lead them into unacceptable behaviors. Through wise discipline and appropriate encouragement, we can help them to learn from their times of brokenness and do better.

•••••••••••

"Trials are medicines which our gracious and wise physician prescribes because we need them; and he proportions the frequency and weight of them to what the case requires."
—JOHN NEWTON, FROM *HEROES OF THE FAITH*

PRAYER: Lord, let Your holiness cover ____ and let (him/her) demonstrate Christ-like behavior to glorify You. When (his/her) spirit is broken, draw (him/her) to You with a contrite heart. In Jesus' name, amen.

*Cleanse me with hyssop, and I will be clean;
wash me, and I will be whiter than snow.*
—PSALM 51:7

Have you ever prayed this prayer?

Teens sometimes feel that their sin is too great and that they are unworthy of mercy. Hearing others confess their sins and receive forgiveness may make it easier for them to do so as well.

• • • • • • • • • •

"From every cut springs new growth."
—ANONYMOUS

PRAYER: Lord, keep____ pure in Your eyes.
Give (him/her) a desire to live a clean life and ask
for forgiveness for sins no matter what the cost.
Let (him/her) see how great Your love and mercy are
and come to You always. In Jesus' name, amen.

*Create in me a pure heart, O God,
    and renew a steadfast spirit within me.
Do not cast me from your presence or take
    your Holy Spirit from me.
Restore to me the joy of your salvation and
    grant me a willing spirit, to sustain me.*
—PSALM 51:10-12

When have you felt you needed to pray a prayer like this? Did you feel that God answered the cry of your heart?

Knowing that God will always cleanse us when we come to Him in repentance and confess our sins renews our hope. When your teen sins, remind him or her that those in the Bible who were chosen by Him still sinned and received God's incredible forgiveness.

• • • • • • • • • •

*"The measure of a man's real character is what he would do
if he knew he would never be found out."*
—THOMAS BABINGTON MACAULAY, FROM *GREAT INSPIRATIONAL QUOTES*

PRAYER: Lord, renew in ___ a steadfast heart.
Restore to (him/her) the joy of Your salvation and
grant that (he/she) may have a willing spirit to accept
Your discipline. In Jesus' name, amen.

DAY
4

*O LORD, do not forsake me; be not
far from me, O my God.*
—PSALM 38:21

Have you ever felt that God had forsaken you? Why?

Trusting in the Lord takes faith. Once a teen learns to trust that God is always with them, he or she can know that confidence comes from God's promise to us, and then follow through knowing He will never leave them.

• • • • • • • • • • •

*"God gives us the vision, then He takes us down to the valley to
batter us into the shape of the vision, and it is in the valley that
so many of us faint and give way. Every vision will be made real
if we will have patience. . . . Let Him put you on His wheel and
whirl you as He likes, and as sure as God is God and you are you,
you will turn out exactly in accordance with the vision."*
—OSWALD CHAMBERS, FROM *MY UTMOST FOR HIS HIGHEST*

PRAYER: Lord, never forsake ___, but help
(him/her) to have a steadfast belief that You
are there no matter what the situation.
Even if (his/her) sin is shameful, urge (him/her)
to come to You, remembering that You are
the all-forgiving God. In Jesus' name, amen.

Have mercy on me, O God, according to your unfailing love; according to your great compassion blot out my transgressions. Wash away all my iniquity and cleanse me from my sin.
—PSALM 51:12

Have you ever experienced God's washing away your iniquity? How did you feel?

Nothing of this earth can bring us the true peace that we find when God washes us clean. Keeping that memory fresh will help teens to stay close to God and to return when they drift away.

· · · · · · · · · · ·

"Faith must be tested, because it can be turned into a personal possession only through conflict. . . . The final thing is confidence in Jesus. Believe steadfastly on Him and all you come up against will develop your faith. . . . Faith is unutterable trust in God, trust which never dreams that He will not stand by us."
—OSWALD CHAMBERS, FROM *PATCHES OF GODLIGHT*

PRAYER: Lord, have mercy upon ___ and blot out all (his/her) transgressions. Remind (him/her) to always come to You to confess even the ugliest of sins and know they are forgiven. In Jesus' name, amen.

I wait for you, O LORD; you will answer, O Lord my God.
—PSALM 38:15

Have you ever prayed and forgotten to wait for an answer?

As we put our mind on God, we receive His wise guidance for every situation. Teach teens by your example to wait on God instead of looking for earthly answers in others and in the temporary fixes offered by this world. God's timing may take longer, but healing for our brokenness is found nowhere else.

PEACE FOR PARENTS OF TEENS

• • • • • • • • • •

"When the going gets rough, the tough get going.""
—ROBERT SCHULLER, FROM *WISE WORDS AND QUOTES*

> PRAYER: Lord, teach ___ to be persistent in prayer
> and to look expectantly for Your answers instead
> of to the things of this world that end up being
> deceptive. Hold (him/her) accountable to You.
> In Jesus' name, amen.

O LORD, open my lips, and my mouth
will declare your praise.
—PSALM 51:15

When God cleanses us, what response comes from our lips?

When God saves us, He makes our broken places whole again. The response to this cleansing is always praise. Teens who have this experience will naturally give their Savior praise and glory.

• • • • • • • • • •

How sweet the name of Jesus sounds
In a believer's ear.
It soothes his sorrows, heals his wounds
And drives away his fear.
—JOHN NEWTON, FROM *HEROES OF THE FAITH*

> PRAYER: Lord, open ___'s lips so (he/she) can
> declare Your praise. Give (him/her) the confidence
> to spread Your gospel among others with words
> that are wise. In Jesus' name, amen.

Week 28
PRIDE

<table>
<tr><td>

DAY
1

</td><td>

For he who avenges blood remembers;
he does not ignore the cry of the afflicted.
—Psalm 9:12

</td></tr>
</table>

Can you seek vengeance on someone if you're humble? How?

Human vengeance arises out of pride, but God's vengeance comes from His justice. Teens often want to take revenge on those who disrespect or treat them badly, but God calls us to turn the other cheek and leave vengeance to Him because only He can judge justly. What kind of example are you giving your teens in this matter?

• • • • • • • • • • •

"A bold Christian is the highest style of a man."
—Thomas Young, from *Patches of Godlight*

> Prayer: Lord, let ___ be obedient to You.
> Let (him/her) follow, revere and serve You.
> Even when (he/she) wants to take matters
> into (his/her) own hands, remind (him/her) that
> You will bring justice in due time.
> In Jesus' name, amen.

He guides the humble in what is right
and teaches them his way.
—PSALM 25:9

How does the Lord guide you to be humble, or can you become humble on your own?

Teens may not be clear about the calling they have from God. The enticements of our society and the pressures of school, activities, and peers can block discernment. They need to develop the humility to stop and listen for God's still, small voice.

• • • • • • • • • • •

"Preach the gospel all the time.
If necessary, use words."
—FRANCIS OF ASSISI, FROM *CHRISTIANITY TODAY*

PRAYER: Lord, give ____ a spirit of teachability.
Make (him/her) willing to humbly learn
from those who are wiser than (him/her).
In Jesus' name, amen.

But the meek will inherit the land
and enjoy great peace.
—PSALMS 37:11

Do you think it makes more sense to say that the strong will inherit the earth? Why or why not?

God's standards are very different from human standards. Power and pride are valued in our society, but not in God's realm. In a teen's world, meekness is usually seen as weakness instead of quiet confidence in a power that is stronger than ours. Help your teen to understand that true strength lies in trusting God, who sees the heart of each person, to bring both justice and mercy.

• • • • • • • • • • •

"To have what we want is riches;
but to be able to do without is power."
—GEORGE MACDONALD, FROM *WIKI QUOTE*

PRAYER: Lord, give ___ the desire to serve others and
a willingness to help those in need. Show (him/her)
the benefit of being strong in silence until others see
(his/her) quiet wisdom and come forth to learn from
(him/her). In Jesus' name, amen.

When pride comes, then comes disgrace,
but with humility comes wisdom.
—PROVERBS 11:2

How can pride bring disgrace and wisdom come from humility?

We have all seen people fall from grace when they become proud. For teens, pride may seem like a positive characteristic. Being proud often exudes confidence in a job well done, but the pride God speaks of is the kind that puts us on a pedestal from which we will surely fall.

• • • • • • • • • • •

"God endows us with gifts so we can make him known."
—MAX LUCADO, FROM *CURE FOR THE COMMON LIFE*

PRAYER: Lord, let godly wisdom enter ___'s heart.
Don't let (him/her) get caught in the trap
of pride that leads to disgrace.
In Jesus' name, amen.

"Has not my hand made all these things, and so they came into being?" declares the LORD. "This is the one I esteem: he who is humble and contrite in spirit, and trembles at my word."
—ISAIAH 66:2

If you do not get credit for achievements, what do you get credit for?

What an incredible thought it is to be esteemed by God. What must one do to achieve such a blessing? He tells us to be humble and contrite, two things that teens often think show weakness and might make them vulnerable.

• • • • • • • • • •

"Almighty and eternal God, so draw my heart to you, so guide my mind, so fill my imagination, so control my will, but I may be wholly yours, utterly dedicated unto you. And then use me, I pray, as you will, and always to your glory, and the welfare of your people. Through our Lord and Savior Jesus Christ. Amen."
—ANONYMOUS

> PRAYER: Lord, let ___ be humble and contrite in spirit. Let (him/her) serve others as if they were You and be esteemed in Your eyes. In Jesus' name, amen.

Take my yoke upon you and learn from me, for I am gentle and humble in heart, and you will find rest for your souls.
—MATTHEW 11:29

Describe how you feel when you turn to God. Are you afraid of His judgment, or do you feel peace in His presence?

To fear God is to feel a reverent awe, not to be frightened. Discuss this difference with your teen so (he/she) will feel comfortable in coming to God for strength or forgiveness.

• • • • • • • • • •

"Jesus is everything."
—MOTHER TERESA, FROM *HEROES OF THE FAITH*

PRAYER: Lord, let ___ take Your yoke and learn
from You. Let (him/her) find rest in
Your presence. In Jesus' name, amen.

*Now that I, your LORD and Teacher, have washed
your feet, you also should wash one another's feet.*
—JOHN 13:14

Would you actually wash someone else's feet?

It takes complete humility to kneel and wash another person's feet, especially if he or she is a stranger or someone you don't really like. Have you modeled this behavior for your teen by literally washing someone's feet or by a similar act of service? How can they learn to humble themselves as Christ did if you aren't willing to do so?

• • • • • • • • • •

*"If we do not radiate the light of Christ around us, the sense of
the darkness that prevails in the world will increase."*
—MOTHER TERESA, FROM *NO GREATER LOVE*

PRAYER: Lord, give ___ the integrity to set a good
example. Help (him/her) to think of ways to "wash
the feet" of others, learning to put others before self.
In Jesus' name, amen.

Week 29

THANKFULNESS

DAY
1

Now, our God, we give you thanks,
and praise your glorious name.
—1 CHRONICLES 29:13

Is it easy for you to be thankful, or do you find yourself taking things for granted often? What is the difference between thanking God and praising Him?

We need to be an example to our teens, demonstrating that being a Christian brings joy even in times of hardship. This isn't an easy task, especially when the hardship involves the teen, but giving thanks for your teen and praising God for the good things he or she does will help you to keep your perspective.

• • • • • • • • • • • •

"Example is not the main thing in influencing others.
It is the only thing."
—ALBERT SCHWEITZER, FROM *MEDITATIONS FOR PARENTS WHO DO TOO MUCH*

PRAYER: Lord, let ____ be thankful for all
Your triumphs and for the victories still in store.
Help (him/her) never to give up hope in You.
In Jesus' name, amen.

I will give you thanks in the great assembly,
among throngs of people I will praise you.
—PSALM 35:18

Do you find it easy or hard to give thanks to God in public?

Teens might not always be joyful in what they do, but they can always be thankful for what the Lord does. Holding on to faith in God will see them through their times of weakness and help them to find strength in Him.

• • • • • • • • • • •

"All heaven and earth resound with that subtle
and delicately balanced truth that the old paths
are the best paths after all."
—J. C. RYLE, FROM *PATCHES OF GODLIGHT*

PRAYER: Lord, let ___ give thanks for all
(his/her) blessings before Your people.
Teach (him/her) Your humble ways and forgiving
heart. Help (him/her) grow to be like You.
In Jesus' name, amen.

We give thanks to you, O God,
we give thanks, for your name is near;
men tell of your wonderful deeds.
—PSALM 75:1

Have you ever been blessed when someone thanked God publicly?

Giving thanks regardless of their circumstances will help teens to stand for God and not be ashamed of their faith. Godly friends who tell of God's wonderful deeds in their own lives will provide the encouragement they need. So will being a godly friend to others.

• • • • • • • • • • •

"Grace is indeed needed to turn a man into a saint; and he who doubts it does not know what a saint or a man is."
—BLAISE PASCAL, FROM *THOUGHTS AND QUOTES*

PRAYER: Lord, remind ___ of all the wonders
You have done. Give (him/her) the words to share
these great works with others and not be
embarrassed in doing so. In Jesus' name, amen.

*Praise the LORD. Give thanks to the LORD,
for he is good; his love endures forever.*
—PSALMS 106:1

Is it easier for you to thank God or to praise him? How do you praise God?

Forever is too great a concept for most teens to grasp. It's the day by day that they remember. Taking God's commands one day, one moment at a time is sometimes all they can do without becoming overwhelmed.

• • • • • • • • • • •

*Love so amazing, so divine,
Demands my soul, my life, my all.*
—ISAAC WATTS, FROM "WHEN I SURVEY THE WONDROUS CROSS"

PRAYER: Lord, let ___ experience the truth that
You are good and that Your love for (him/her)
endures forever. In Jesus' name, amen.

*But thanks be to God that, though you used to be
slaves to sin, you wholeheartedly obeyed the form
of teaching to which you were entrusted.*
—ROMANS 6:17

Have you ever thought of yourself as a slave to sin? What sin are you no longer a slave to because of God?

Freedom is something we so easily take for granted until it is taken from us. When teens are in bondage to sin, it can be difficult for us to understand what they are going through or how we can help. Only God can give us guidance to bridge the gap.

• • • • • • • • • • •

May the grace of Christ our Savior
and the Father's boundless love
with the Holy Spirit's favor,
rest upon us from above.

Thus we make abide in union
with each other and the Lord,
and possess, in sweet communion,
joy which Earth cannot afford.
—JOHN NEWTON, FROM *HEROES OF THE FAITH*

PRAYER: Lord, release ___ from the bondage of sin and free (him/her) to wholeheartedly obey You. In Jesus' name, amen.

DAY
6

. . . always giving thanks to God the Father
for everything, in the name of our Lord Jesus Christ.
—EPHESIANS 5:20

Do we have to thank God for everything? Don't we get credit for anything?

It's tempting for teens to think they are responsible for their successes and forget to thank God. Remembering where true power comes from and thanking God for His undeserved favor will keep them from stumbling.

• • • • • • • • • • •

*"Be careful for nothing, prayerful for everything,
thankful for anything."*
—DWIGHT L. MOODY, FROM *HEROES OF THE FAITH*

PRAYER: Lord, manifest in ___ the sweet aroma of the
knowledge of You. Let it linger to help (him/her) to
serve you with thanksgiving. In Jesus' name, amen.

DAY
7

*Do not be anxious about anything, but in everything,
by prayer and petition, with thanksgiving,
present your requests to God.*
—PHILIPPIANS 4:6

**Do you thank God when you pray about something, or do
you wait for His answer first?**

Putting prayer in the place of worry can do much for the soul.
When your teen is anxious about something, does he or she
turn it over to God in prayer and thanksgiving? When one experiences the relief of relinquishing a burden to the Lord, it becomes
easier to go to Him right away the next time instead of worrying.

• • • • • • • • • • •

*"I have a great need for Christ.
I have a great Christ for my need."*
—CHARLES H. SPURGEON, FROM *HEROES OF THE FAITH*

PRAYER: Lord, help ___ to recognize all Your
blessings and be thankful for them. Teach (him/her)
to come to you right away in times of difficulty
and trust you to supply the need.
In Jesus' name, amen.

*For this reason a man will leave his father
and mother and be united to his wife,
and they will become one flesh.*
—GENESIS 2:24

**What are the good and the difficult things that can happen
when a man or woman leaves the family to get married?**

Leaving one's family to form another allows the cycle of life
to remain unbroken. This is nature's way and God's plan to
grow teens into responsible adults. And as they mature and
become independent, the extended family provides needed
support to raise the next generation.

• • • • • • • • • • •

*"The linking of generations, the historical lineage of family,
the sharing of love give purpose to life."*
—GEORGE LANDBERG, FROM *FAMILY TREE MAGAZINE*

PRAYER: Lord, show ___ that You have created
our family to nurture him or her until he or she
is grown and able to create his or her own family.
Help ___ to be obedient to us and to You.
In Jesus' name, amen.

Only be careful, and watch yourselves closely so that you do not forget the things your eyes have seen or let them slip from your heart as long as you live. Teach them to your children and to their children after them.
—DEUTERONOMY 4:9

What things have you learned that you will teach your children and grandchildren?

The legacy you leave will make an impact on many—not just your own teens but also their children after them. God calls us to remember His blessings and faithfully teach our children about Him so they will pass the knowledge of God to their children.

• • • • • • • • • •

"It isn't easy growing up in today's world. Pressures to conform, to be 'in', 'with it'. Pressures to rebel. A materialistic, secular society and the false standard created by it. There are no morals left in the world. Instead of "Thou shall not," it is "Why not?"
—RUTH BELL GRAHAM, FROM *BLESSINGS FOR A MOTHER'S DAY*

PRAYER: Lord, may ___ hold in (his/her) heart all Your teachings and not forget Your faithfulness. Help (him/her) to pass on these lessons to (his/her) children. In Jesus' name, amen.

"But if serving the LORD becomes undesirable to you, then choose for yourselves this day whom you will serve, whether the gods your forefathers served beyond the River, or the gods of the Amorites, in whose land you are living. But as for me and my household, we will serve the LORD."
—JOSHUA 24:15

How do you answer the challenge given in this verse? How would the two different answers affect your life? Your death?

The calling of God comes with great responsibility. Serving Him requires that we make an active choice to live our lives according to God's will. Teens who choose to follow Jesus early in their lives often demonstrate more passion and energy for God than adults who have been church members for a long time, but they can also quickly become disillusioned. What kind of example are you giving them?

• • • • • • • • • •

"This is what I found out about religion: It gives you courage
to make decisions you must make in a crisis,
and then the confidence to leave the result
to a Higher Power."
—DWIGHT D. EISENHOWER, FROM *QUOTATION COLLECTION*

PRAYER: Lord, help ___ to choose to serve
You and not the alluring gods of this world.
In Jesus' name, amen.

DAY 4

She watches over the affairs of her household
and does not eat the bread of idleness.
—PROVERBS 31:27

If you were teaching this verse to your daughter, what message would your life give her?

It is easy for teens to get caught up in laziness and gossip. The best way to teach teens to persevere in godly living is to let them see it in your life. Actions speak louder than words. Teens notice whether the people around them do what they say they will and live according to what they say they believe.

• • • • • • • • • •

"It is impossible to enjoy idling thoroughly
unless one has plenty of work to do."
—JEROME K. JEROME, FROM *PATCHES OF GODLIGHT*

PRAYER: Lord, teach ___ the value of honest work.
Inspire (him/her) not to be idle but to do all things
for Your glory. In Jesus' name, amen.

*He and all his family were devout and
God-fearing; he gave generously to those
in need and prayed to God regularly.*
—ACTS 10:2

Do people say this about you and your family? What might you have to work on?

This is a lot to live up to, but a worthy goal for all of us who fear the Lord. If our teens see us giving generously to those in need and praying regularly, it will make a deep impression that will last all their lives.

· · · · · · · · · · ·

*"The only rock I know that stays steady, the only
institution I know that works, is the family."*
—LEE IACOCCA, FROM *FINEST QUOTES*

PRAYER: Lord, let ___ see the need for us
to nurture what God has entrusted to us: our family.
Help (him/her) to see how important family is
and not to stray too far. Keep (him/her) always
with You when (he/she) seeks out independence.
In Jesus' name, amen.

*Husbands love your wives, just as Christ loved the
church and gave himself up for her.*
—EPHESIANS 5:25

To daughter: Would you want to be married to someone who didn't love you as Christ loves the church? To son: Will you choose to love your wife in this way?

Conflicts will inevitably arise when two people live together. We're human, and we want our own way. But when we love as Christ loves us, we choose to set aside our selfish desires for the good of the other. It is the highest form of love and a powerful lesson for our children to carry with them into their own marriage relationship.

• • • • • • • • • • •

"Husbands who realize that others need to first feel understood before they can listen to a different perspective elicit a great deal of respect from their wives. They also become very proficient problem solvers and peacemakers."
—James Dobson, from *365 Day Brighteners to Warm Your Home*

PRAYER: Lord, let ___ find a mate
with whom (he/she) can be perfectly joined
so that they might edify each other. Keep (him/her)
from those who may excite, but who stray
from Your path. Hold (him/her) close together
with (his/her) chosen one in Your binding love
for all their lives. In Jesus' name, amen.

DAY
7

He must manage his own family well and see that his children obey him with proper respect.
—1 Timothy 3:4

What do you think are the best ways to teach your children to obey and respect you?

Teen don't have enough experience in life to see things from a parent's perspective. By explaining the reasons behind your rules and being open to working out a reasonable compromise when possible, you may be able to minimize times of rebellion.

• • • • • • • • • • •

*"Training children involves helping them shape
their ambitions and their sense of personal destiny."*
—GORDON MCDONALD, FROM *365 DAY BRIGHTENERS TO WARM YOUR HOME*

PRAYER: Lord, help ___ to see that parents
understand things they can't, and that our decisions
are meant for their good. Help us as parents to set
reasonable rules and be wise in our discipline.
In Jesus' name, amen.

Week 31

JUSTIFICATION

| DAY |
| 1 |

This is what the LORD says, "Maintain justice and do what is right, for my salvation is close at hand and my righteousness will soon be revealed."
—ISAIAH 56:1

How hard is it for you to maintain justice and do what is right?

If it's hard for us as adults to always be just and do what is right, how can we expect our teens to be perfect? We need to remember that our young people haven't yet gained the experience and knowledge that we have. Being just with our teens means keeping this in mind as we set boundaries for them and administer discipline when they break the rules.

• • • • • • • • • • •

"You cannot be anything you want to be. But you can be everything God wants you to be."
—MAX LUCADO, FROM *CURE FOR THE COMMON LIFE*

PRAYER: Lord, give me insight and wisdom
in dealing with ___. Help me to teach (him/her)
Your ways with patience and love.
In Jesus' name, amen.

I tell you the truth, whoever hears my word and believes him who sent me has eternal life and will not be condemned; he has crossed over from death to life.
—JOHN 5:24

Have you committed your life to Christ? Has your teen?

It's possible to listen without really hearing. I'm sure you've had that experience with your teen from time to time, and if we're honest, God probably has that experience with us on occasion too! Before our teens can understand that Jesus is the Way, the Truth, and the Life, they have to hear the gospel. Do you make Bible study a regular part of your family life?

● ● ● ● ● ● ● ● ● ●

"Every child is shaped by the mind of God."
—ANONYMOUS

PRAYER: Lord, help ___ to understand that (he/she) can be forgiven and justified only by believing in You. In Jesus' name, amen.

This righteousness from God comes through faith in Jesus Christ to all who believe. There is no difference, for all have sinned and fall short of the glory of God, and are justified freely by his grace through the redemption that came by Christ Jesus.
—ROMANS 3:22–24

Can you feel righteous without feeling proud?

Righteousness is not something we can achieve by our own efforts. We are saved by faith, not by works so that we will have nothing to boast about. Jesus did it all. When teens truly understand that their sins are forgiven and they are justified by God's grace through Jesus' death on the cross, they will be freed from the frustration and discouragement of trying to earn salvation.

• • • • • • • • • • •

"The Christian way is different: harder, and easier.
Christ says, 'Give me All. I don't want so much of your time
and so much of your money and so much of your work:
I want You. I have not come to torment your natural self,
but to kill it. No half-measures are any good. I don't want
to cut off a branch here and a branch there, I want to have the
whole tree down. . . . Hand over the whole natural self, all the
desires which you think innocent as well as the ones you think
wicked—the whole outfit. I will give you a new self instead. In
fact, I will give you Myself: my own will shall become yours.'"
—C. S. Lewis, from *Mere Christianity*

PRAYER: Lord, help ___ to understand that (he/she)
can be forgiven and justified only by believing
in You. In Jesus' name, amen.

DAY
4

Therefore, since we have been justified
through faith, we have peace with God
through our Lord Jesus Christ.
—Romans 5:1

What does justification mean? What is the result of our justification?

When we accept Jesus as our Savior, God justifies us. That means He judges us to be righteous and worthy of salvation. It is this work of God that sets us in a relationship of peace with Him. By helping our teens to grasp this concept, we should see spiritual fruit begin to develop in their lives.

• • • • • • • • • • •

"There has never been such a miracle
as a self-righteous man coming to Christ for mercy;
none but those who want a Savior ever did come."
—Charles H. Spurgeon, from *An Appeal to Sinners*

PRAYER: Lord, cause ___ to long for Your justification,
to choose to be a disciple of Jesus and live for You.
In Jesus' name, amen.

*Consequently, just as the result of one trespass
was condemnation for all men, so also the result
of one act of righteousness was justification
that brings life for all men.*
—ROMANS 5:18

Who was the first person referred to here? Who is the second one? What did they do?

Knowing Adam was the first to fail can help teens realize they were condemned to sin before they were ever born. More important, they should know that their Savior died because of that first sin, and also for their sins. As a result, God's justification is available to bring them new life.

• • • • • • • • • • •

*"Only someone with a broken heart
would want to mend broken legs and wings.*
—JILL BRISCOE, FROM *GOD'S FRONT DOOR*

PRAYER: Lord, let ___ know that You are the great
revival and You will restore us. Nothing (he/she)
can do will ever be too much for Christ to forgive.
In Jesus' name, amen.

*Who will bring any charge against those
whom God has chosen? It is God who justifies.*
—ROMANS 8:33

Does this verse mean that God approves our behavior when we break His laws? Does it mean that we won't suffer the consequences of our sin?

Justification doesn't mean that God overlooks our sin or shields us from its consequences. It does mean that we are no longer under condemnation and are now able to live at peace with God. Teens need to know that they have this unconditional love from their heavenly Father, and that although they will have to face the consequences for their wrong actions, God will be there to help them through it.

• • • • • • • • • •

"A man's spiritual health is exactly proportional to his love for God."
—C. S. LEWIS, FROM *IN PURSUIT OF TRUTH*

PRAYER: Lord, help ___ to trust in You when (he/she) suffers the consequences of sin. When the Evil One accuses, help ___ to know that (he/she) is no longer under condemnation, but is justified by You.
In Jesus' name, amen.

DAY
7

For it is with your heart that you believe and are justified, and it is with your mouth that you confess and are saved.
—ROMANS 10:10

Why do we need to both believe with our heart and confess with our mouth?

Belief springs from the heart, or spirit. But simply believing is not enough. We want our teens to also openly confess their sins and receive pardon, and then confess their new faith as a testimony to others. When we speak what we believe, we make ourselves accountable to live a life consistent with our words.

• • • • • • • • • •

"Faith in a God big enough and near enough and powerful enough to teach me how to trust and not be aftaid."
—JILL BRISCOE, FROM *GOD'S FRONT DOOR*

PRAYER: Lord, help ___ to believe in Your Son Jesus, to confess (his/her) sins, and to tell others about You in sweet and loving words that draw them to You. In Jesus' name, amen.

Week 32
FORGIVE

A man's wisdom gives him patience;
it is to his glory to overlook an offense.
—Proverbs 19:11

Do you admire someone who overlooks an offense?

Teens may view patience and the willingness to overlook offenses as weakness. By pointing out these qualities in people they are familiar with from the Bible, history, and the present day, you can help them to learn that self-control is really the evidence of true wisdom and strength.

• • • • • • • • • • •

"He who runs from God in the morning will
scarcely find him the rest of the day."
—John Bunyan, from *Heroes of the Faith*

PRAYER: Lord, give ___ the patience to calm
quarrels by holding (his/her) tongue when tempted
to use harsh words. Help him/her) to overlook
the offense when (his/her) heart is pierced.
In Jesus' name, amen.

DAY

2

*Forgive us our debts, as we also have
forgiven our debtors.*
—MATTHEW 6:12

How do you come out in this comparison?

God forgives us as we forgive others, even when they don't deserve it, just as we don't deserve God's mercy. Do you forgive your teen when he or she behaves badly, or do you remind him or her often of the offense? The way we treat our teens will determine to a large degree how they will treat their own children.

• • • • • • • • • • •

*"A great many people are trying to make
their peace with God, but that has already
been done. God has not left it for us to do;
all we have to do is to enter into it."*
—DWIGHT L. MOODY, FROM *HEROES OF THE FAITH*

PRAYER: Lord, let ____ judge impartially,
just as You do. Let (him/her) see the wonders mercy
can bring to a person who feels condemned.
Let (him/her) feel Your mighty hand on (him/her)
and make (him/her) white as snow.
In Jesus' name, amen.

DAY

3

*For if you forgive men when they sin against you,
your heavenly Father will also forgive you.*
—MATTHEW 6:14

Do you expect others to forgive you in the same way you forgive them? Would you want them to?

Being forgiven by God places the burden of forgiving others on us. If Jesus died on the cross to forgive our sins, then how can we remain hard-hearted toward others? How can we remain hard-hearted toward our teens?

• • • • • • • • • •

*"Forgiveness is not an emotion. . . . Forgiveness is
an act of the will, and the will can function regardless
of the temperature of the heart."*
—CORRIE TEN BOOM, FROM *HEROES OF THE FAITH*

PRAYER: Lord, give ___ the grace to forgive others
and the contrite heart to ask for forgiveness
when necessary. Help me to be a good example
to (him/her) by the way I forgive.
In Jesus' name, amen.

DAY 4

*Then Peter came to Jesus and asked, "LORD, how many
times shall I forgive my brother when he sins against
me? Up to seven times?" Jesus answered, "I tell you,
not seven times, but seventy-seven times."*
—MATTHEW 18:21

**Is it realistic for you to obey this verse? How can you forgive
someone seventy-seven times without teaching them that
their behavior is okay?**

Only the power of God's love makes it possible for us to obey
this command. Forgiveness doesn't imply that the one who
forgives approves of the offense or that the wrongdoer won't suffer the consequences of the action. Under some circumstances,
such as physical or sexual abuse, it may not be possible to continue the relationship. We need to make sure our teens understand that. But forgiving frees us from the bondage of anger and
allows God to work in the situation.

• • • • • • • • • •

*"A man there was, though some did count him mad,
the more he cast away, the more he had."*
—FROM *PILGRIM'S PROGRESS* BY JOHN BUNYAN

PRAYER: Lord, let ___ see how a forgiving attitude can
free (him/her) of anger and resentment and turn it
into mercy. In Jesus' name, amen.

**DAY
5**

*And when you stand praying, if you hold anything
against anyone, forgive him, so that your Father in
heaven may forgive you.*
—MARK 11:25

Is forgiving those who have offended you a regular part of your prayer time?

It's easy to allow a grudge to fester unless we make it a practice to express forgiveness in our prayers. That includes forgiving ourselves for sins God has cleansed us of. Encourage your teen to forgive him or herself as well as others through prayer.

• • • • • • • • • • •

*"We must lay before him what is in us,
not what ought to be in us."*
—C. S. LEWIS, FROM *HEROES OF THE FAITH*

PRAYER: Lord, let ___ have a heart to forgive others
as You forgive (him/her). Help (him/her) to
lay aside the things that are past and claim
Your cleansing for (his/her) sins.
In Jesus' name, amen.

**DAY
6**

*But love your enemies, do good to them,
and lend to them without expecting to get anything
back. Then your reward will be great, and you
will be sons of the Most High, because he is
kind to the ungrateful and wicked.*
—LUKE 6:35

If you do what Jesus commands in this verse, will your enemies remain enemies—or will you begin to look at them as friends?

What a surprise our enemies would have if we lived this out! As parents, we can encourage our teens to do what the Lord asks of them and see what changes it makes in their relationships. They might be surprised too.

• • • • • • • • • • •

"Love accepts the trying things of life without asking for explanations. It trusts and is at rest."
—AMY CARMICHAEL, FROM *HEROES OF THE FAITH*

PRAYER: Lord, instill in ___ a heart to love (his/her) enemies and do good to them, just as You are kind to the ungrateful and wicked. Pour on (him/her) the blessings that result from obedience.
In Jesus' name, amen.

DAY 7

Jesus said, "Father, forgive them, for they do not know what they are doing." And they divided up his clothes by casting lots.
—LUKE 23:34

Would you forgive someone who tried to kill you and even took your clothing in the attempt?

When someone attacks us or a loved one, it's hard to forgive. Even harder is to forgive someone who murders a child. Jesus forgave those who nailed him to the cross, and then divided his clothing while he suffered, and he commanded us to do the same. Parents who forgive their child's murderer and seek to win him or her to Christ are powerful examples for us and our teens of God's love in action.

• • • • • • • • • • •

"When God forgives he forgets. He buries our sins in the seas and puts up a sign on the shore saying, 'No fishing allowed.'"
—CORRIE TEN BOOM, FROM *HEROES OF THE FAITH*

PRAYER: Lord, teach ___ to forgive as You forgive, even when the offense is great. Give (him/her) Your mind to follow You in all things. In Jesus' name, amen.

Week 33
INTEGRITY

He who has clean hands and a pure heart . . .
will receive blessing from the LORD and
vindication from God his Savior.
—PSALMS 24:4A-5

What makes a person trustworthy?

It may be hard for a teen to continue to act with integrity when peers don't. But the Bible promises that the Lord will bless and vindicate those who do what is right from a pure heart, and that's an assurance that will carry teens through times of disillusionment and doubt.

• • • • • • • • • • •

"The world has always been betrayed
by decent men with bad ideals."
—SYDNEY J. HARRIS, FROM *PATCHES OF GODLIGHT*

PRAYER: Lord, let ___ find friends who support (him/her) in acting with integrity. Let (him/her) be the one others turn to who seek to know You.
In Jesus' name, amen.

DAY 2

The man of integrity walks securely, but he who takes crooked paths will be found out.
—PROVERBS 10:9

Is it possible to hide sin from God?

Have you noticed that secret sin almost always comes to light. Pointing out examples of this truth in news accounts about famous people can help to encourage our teens to walk a straight path. They also need to be reminded that even if no one else knows their sin, God does. The Bible promises that when we act with integrity, God will make our path secure, and we need to pray that our teens heed that message.

•••••••••••

"I realized then that I already know most of what's necessary to live a meaningful life, that it isn't all that complicated. I know it. And have known it for a long, long time. Living it, well that's another matter, yes?"
—ROBERT FULGHUM, FROM *ALL I REALLY NEED TO KNOW I LEARNED IN KINDERGARTEN*

PRAYER: Lord, when ___ stumbles, cause (him/her) to take Your hand and allow You to lead (him/her) in a secure path. In Jesus' name, amen.

DAY 3

The integrity of the upright guides them, but the unfaithful are destroyed by their duplicity.
—PROVERBS 11:3

In what situations is it easy for you to act with integrity? When is it hard to be honest?

According to the dictionary, one meaning of integrity is to be complete or undivided, whereas duplicity is contradictory doubleness of thought, speech, or action. That makes it easy to see why being dishonest is the recipe for destruction. Do you guide your teen with integrity and uprightness? If we are unfaithful in our parenting, we're setting our teens up for destruction.

• • • • • • • • • •

"Character is made by many acts: it may be lost by a single act."
—Anonymous, from *Wise Words and Quotes*

> PRAYER: Lord, help ___ to be honorable in all (he/she) does. Let (his/her) heart be undivided and wholly dedicated to You. In Jesus' name, amen.

DAY 4

He who walks righteously and speaks what is right, who rejects gain from extortion and keeps his hand from accepting bribes, who stops his ears against plots of murder and shuts his eyes against contemplating evil—this is the man who will dwell on the heights, whose refuge will be the mountain fortress. His bread will be supplied, and water will not fail him.
—Isaiah 33:15-16

Do you always strive to do the right thing, or are there times when you fudge, cheat, fabricate, exaggerate, misrepresent, and distort . . . just a little?

It's tempting to fudge the truth just a little when the stakes are high and the lie seems so small. But what would it be like if God cheated, fabricated, or distorted His truth even slightly? Can we even imagine it? In our world, we represent God to our children. If our teens see us acting unrighteously, it's the same for them as if God cheated.

• • • • • • • • • •

"Human excellence means nothing unless it works with the consent of God.
—Euripides, from *Wise Words and Quotes*

PRAYER: Lord, cause ___ to walk righteously
before You and reject evil in all (he/she) does.
Let (him/her dwell on the heights and find
a refuge in You. In Jesus' name, amen.

DAY
5

Do to others as you would have them do to you.
—LUKE 6:31

Do you treat others as you want them to treat you? What changes would you have to make to do this?

Integrity requires that we treat others the way we want them to treat us. Teens may feel anxious about doing this because they fear that their peers might not respond in kind. It may take time for them to make a positive impact on their peer group, but if they stand firm, they will turn enemies into friends.

• • • • • • • • • •

*"You cannot do a kindness too soon, for you
never know how soon it will be too late."*
—RALPH W. EMERSON, FROM *PATCHES OF GODLIGHT*

PRAYER: Lord, give ___ the maturity to treat others
as (he/she) wants to be treated. Strengthen (him/her)
in times of trouble, and let (him/her) experience
positive changes in relationships as a result.
In Jesus' name, amen.

DAY
6

*"I strive always to keep my conscience
clear before God and man."*
—ACTS 24:16

Is it possible to lie to your conscience?

Sometimes we get caught up in a web of our own lies. Lying is harder than telling the truth because we tend to forget the details of the story we told. Sooner or later, our lies will trap us. Make sure you always tell your teen the truth and expect the same from him or her.

• • • • • • • • • • •

"No legacy is so rich as honesty."
—FROM *ALL'S WELL THAT ENDS WELL* BY WILLIAM SHAKESPEARE

PRAYER: Lord, let ___ see through the trap of lying. Help (him/her) to always keep (his/her) conscience clear before You and others. In Jesus' name, amen.

DAY 7

They must keep hold of the deep truths of the faith with a clear conscience.
—1 TIMOTHY 3:9

What does it mean to have a clear conscience? Is it possible to keep hold of the deep truths of the faith if your conscience isn't clear?

In today's world a clear conscience isn't valued very much. As in the Book of Judges, most people do whatever seems right in their own eyes, with no thought for God's laws. We need to instill in our teens a solid understanding of God's Word so they will choose to keep hold of the deep truths of the faith along with a clear conscience.

• • • • • • • • • • •

"Dare to be honest and fear no labor."
—ROBERT BURNS, FROM *PATCHES OF GODLIGHT*

PRAYER: Lord, help ___ to be truthful in all things. If (he/she) sins, help (him/her) to confess, ask pardon, and receive forgiveness from You and from all those who have been offended. In Jesus' name, amen.

Week 34
WATCH

DAY 1

Only be careful, and watch yourselves closely so that you do not forget the things your eyes have seen or let them slip from your heart as long as you live. Teach them to your children and to their children after them.
—DEUTERONOMY 4:9

What are two things you have learned that you really want your children to learn?

It's easy to push past experiences out of our minds, especially if they were painful, but it's important to make an effort to remember the lessons we have learned. Sharing your experiences can open your teen's eyes to dangers they may not recognize and also guide him or her in making positive choices for the future.

· · · · · · · · · · ·

"There are times when fear is good. It must keep its watchful place at the heart's controls.
—AESCHYLUS, FROM *FAMOUS QUOTES AND AUTHORS*

PRAYER: Lord, let ___ be open to hearing what we have learned through experience and make wise choices accordingly. In Jesus' name, amen.

199

DAY
2

Set a guard over my mouth, O LORD;
keep watch over the door of my lips.
—PSALM 141:3

What are the things you most need to guard your mouth and lips against? Why is it so hard not to talk with others about them?

All of us at one time or another say something we later regret. Teens often speak impulsively without thinking about the consequences when they need to save face or defend themselves. We can help to guide our teens in learning to guard their mouths and also how to gracefully correct a slip when necessary.

• • • • • • • • • • •

"He speaketh not; and yet there lies
A conversation in his eyes."
—HENRY W. LONGFELLOW, FROM *THE HANGING OF THE CRANE*

PRAYER: Lord, cause ___ to delight in honesty
and always be truthful. Let (his/her) words be
sweet and reflect Your own. Help (him/her) to speak
what is good and not the bad, to overlook
the shortcomings of others and strive to see
their strengths. In Jesus' name, amen.

DAY
3

Above all else, guard your heart,
for it is the wellspring of life.
—PROVERBS 4:23

What does the Bible mean by the word heart? Why is this the wellspring of life?

When the Bible speaks about the heart, it refers to the inmost character, the emotional or moral nature of an individual. The author of Proverbs calls this the wellspring of life because it is the moral nature that governs all our actions and thoughts, and consequently our relationship to God. Teens are especially vulnerable to being lured away from God's path. As parents we have the responsibility of forming their moral nature and teaching them to guard their hearts.

• • • • • • • • • • •

"The enemies of the truth are always awfully nice."
—CHRISTOPHER MORLEY, FROM *PATCHES OF GODLIGHT*

PRAYER: Lord, let ____ listen to wise counsel and guard (his/her) heart. Give me wisdom, insight, and patience as I strive to form (his/her) moral nature according to Your leading.
In Jesus' name, amen.

DAY 4

Blessed is the man who listens to me, watching daily at my doors, waiting at my doorway.
—PROVERBS 8:34

Are you daily listening for what the Lord has to say to you?

Modern life is so busy that we can easily forget to listen for God's voice through regular Bible study and prayer and as a result lose blessings God meant for us. Teens can easily get so caught up in activities and in trying to fit in with their peers that they neglect cultivating a close relationship with the Lord. How can you encourage your teen to watch daily at God's doors?

• • • • • • • • • • •

Watch your thoughts; they become words.
Watch your words; they become actions.
Watch your actions; they become habits.
Watch your habits; they become character.
Watch your character; it becomes your destiny.
—ANONYMOUS

> PRAYER: Lord, give ___ a desire to daily study Your
> Word and pray. Lead (him/her) to depend on You
> for all things and to offer (his/her) life to You
> in trust and faith. In Jesus' name, amen.

DAY 5

"Watch and pray so that you will not fall into temptation. The spirit is willing, but the body is weak."
—MATTHEW 26:41

According to this verse, how can we resist temptation?

Teens' bodies and minds will often battle. They may know what is right but have a hard time following through for many reasons. As parents we can help them to see the consequence of each choice and encourage them to watch for situations in which they're likely to be tempted so they can pray for the strength to resist.

• • • • • • • • • • •

*"The honest man takes pains and then enjoys pleasures.
The knave takes pleasures and then suffers pains."*
—BENJAMIN FRANKLIN, FROM *POOR RICHARD'S ALMANAC*

> PRAYER: Lord, let ___ be watchful when temptation
> comes. Teach (him/her) to guard (his/her) mind
> and soul when feeling the pull to sin and choose
> to turn to You. In Jesus' name, amen.

DAY 6

Therefore, dear friends, since you already know this, be on your guard so that you may not be carried away by the error of lawless men and fall from your secure position.
—2 PETER 3:17

Who in your life do you need to be most cautious of right now? Why do you have to be wary of that person?

We often wish we could protect our teens from people who may hurt them and lead them into error. Teaching them to be discerning about their friends and to learn from past experiences will help to safeguard them from serious mistakes.

• • • • • • • • • • •

"We are perpetually being told . . . that what is wanted is a strong man who will do things. What is wanted is a strong man who will undo things; and that will be a real test of strength."
—G. K. CHESTERTON, FROM *WHAT I SAW IN AMERICA*

PRAYER: Lord, keep ___ from conformity and help (him/her) to avoid deceptive philosophy. Teach ___ to trust what the scriptures say about You, and keep (him/her) from being carried away by the errors of those who hate your laws. In Jesus' name, amen.

DAY 7

Watch out that you do not lose what you have worked for, but that you may be rewarded fully.
—2 JOHN 1:8

What kind of reward can we expect from God?

We won't know the full extent of the rewards God gives those who love Him until we see Him face to face, but we do know the greatest of these is everlasting life. As parents it is our desire to lead our children to accept Jesus as their Savior and follow Him all their lives. We surely do not want to lose our full reward by neglecting our responsibility to be a godly example, to teach them God's truth, and to pray for them daily.

• • • • • • • • • • •

"What you do when you don't have to, determines what you will do when you can no longer help it."
—RUDYARD KIPLING, FROM *PATCHES OF GODLIGHT*

PRAYER: Lord, empower ___ to understand what true love and sacrifice are by what You have done to make (him/her) Yours. In Jesus' name, amen.

Week 35
MIRACLES

DAY
1

When Jesus had entered Capernaum, a centurion came to him, asking for help. " Lord," he said, "my servant lies at home paralyzed and in terrible suffering." Jesus said to him, "I will go and heal him." The centurion replied, "Lord, I do not deserve to have you come under my roof. But just say the word, and my servant will be healed. For I myself am a man under authority, with soldiers under me. I tell this one, 'Go,' and he goes; and that one, 'Come,' and he comes. I say to my servant, 'Do this,' and he does it." When Jesus heard this, he was astonished and said to those following him, "I tell you the truth, I have not found anyone in Israel with such great faith . . . Then Jesus said to the centurion, "Go! It will be done just as you believed it would." And his servant was healed that very hour.
—Matthew 8:5-10, 13

Why did Jesus say the centurion had such great faith? Have you ever prayed for a miracle the way the centurion did?

If only we had faith like the centurion when opposition came our way. It is not only his great faith but also his concern for a lowly servant that makes him so admirable. We need to encourage our teens to be modern-day centurions.

• • • • • • • • • •

*"I do not know how the great loving Father will
bring out light at last, but he knows, and he will do it."*
—DAVID LIVINGSTONE, FROM *AFRICA*

PRAYER: Lord, help ___ to see the wondrous works
You do in our everyday lives. Teach (him/her) to give
You the credit. In Jesus' name, amen.

DAY
2

*As Jesus went on from there, two blind men
followed him, calling out, "Have mercy on us,
son of David!" When he had gone indoors,
the blind men came to him, and he asked them,
"Do you believe that I am able to do this?"
"Yes, LORD," they replied. Then he touched their
eyes and said, "According to your faith will it be
done to you;" and their sight was restored.*
—MATTHEW 9:27-30

**If Jesus were with us today in the flesh, would you have the
faith to believe He can heal you? Do you have as much faith
with him not being physically here? Should we be expected to
have the same faith?**

If only our teens had eyes to see and faith to believe, what
glorious things they would experience! If they will keep
their eyes on Jesus and continue walking in faith, they can
have the assurance that He will perform miracles on their
behalf.

• • • • • • • • • • •

*"Faith, like light, should ever be simple and unbending;
while love, like warmth, should beam forth on every side,
and bend to every necessity of our brethren."*
—MARTIN LUTHER, FROM *HEROES OF THE FAITH*

PRAYER: Lord, establish in ____ a strong faith in You.
Don't let the Evil One's doubt creep in and sway
(him/her) into unbelief. In Jesus' name, amen.

A furious squall came up, and the waves broke over the boat, so that it was nearly swamped. Jesus was in the stern, sleeping on a cushion. The disciples woke him and said to him, "Teacher, don't you care if we drown?" He got up, rebuked the wind and said to the waves, "Quiet! Be still!" Then the wind died down and it was completely calm. He said to his disciples, "Why are you so afraid? Do you still have no faith?" They were terrified and asked each other, "Who is this? Even the wind and the waves obey him!"
—MARK 4:37-41

The disciples struggled with faith even though Jesus was right there with them. If Jesus were right here with you, do you think your faith would be stronger than that of the disciples?

Sometimes Jesus isn't as real to teens as someone physically standing in front of them. Their faith will only grow if they fix their eyes on Him and choose to walk with Him day by day. By sharing our experiences of God's moving in our lives, we can help to strengthen our teens' assurance that Christ is with them too.

• • • • • • • • • • •

"We ought not to tolerate for a minute the ghastly and grievous thought that God will not answer prayer.
—CHARLES SPURGEON, FROM *HEROES OF FAITH*

PRAYER: Lord, give ___ the desire to draw closer
to You. Help ___ to retain Your Word in (his/her)
heart and mind. In Jesus' name, amen.

DAY
4

*Jesus asked the boy's father, "How long has he
been like this?" "From childhood," he answered.
"It has often thrown him into fire or water to kill him.
But if you can do anything, take pity on us and
help us." "'If you can'?" said Jesus. "Everything
is possible for him who believes." Immediately
the boy's father exclaimed, "I do believe;
help me overcome my unbelief!"*
—MARK 9:21-24

**When the father says, "I do believe; help me overcome my
unbelief," what does he mean?**

We know our faith is weak, and Jesus is the only one who
can make it strong again. Being honest about what we are
lacking, just as this father was, will help us and our teens open
ourselves to Jesus' power to work miracles in our lives.

• • • • • • • • • • •

*"You never know how much you really believe
anything until its truth or falsehood becomes
a matter of life and death to you."*
—C. S. LEWIS, FROM *HEROES OF THE FAITH*

PRAYER: Lord, let ___ trust in You in times
of trouble and times of doubt. Help (him/her)
to always go to You first before any human,
so as not to be misled. In Jesus' name, amen.

Some men came carrying a paralytic on a mat and tried to take him into the house to lay him before Jesus. When they could not find a way to do this because of the crowd, they went up on the roof and lowered him on his mat through the tiles into the middle of the crowd, right in front of Jesus. When Jesus saw their faith, he said, "Friend, your sins are forgiven."
—LUKE 5:18-20

What have you been able to do on faith alone?

Love and faithfulness are precious to God and will be rewarded. Going to the lengths these men did may seem overzealous to us, but the miracle Jesus performed because of their faith should encourage us to follow their example.

• • • • • • • • • • •

"As nobody else can go to hell or heaven for me, nobody else can believe or disbelieve for me; as nobody else can open or close heaven or hell to me, so nobody else can drive me to belief or unbelief."
—MARTIN LUTHER, FROM *SELECTED WRITINGS*

PRAYER: Lord, I pray that ___ will be as persistent as these men in coming to You in times of need, regardless of the obstacles that stand in (his/her) way. In Jesus' name, amen.

She came up behind him and touched him and touched the edge of his cloak, and immediately her bleeding stopped. "Who touched me?" Jesus asked. When they all denied it, Peter said, "Master, the people are crowding and pressing against you." But Jesus said, "Someone touched me; I know that power has gone out from me." Then the woman, seeing that she could not go unnoticed, came trembling and fell at

his feet. In the presence of all the people, she told why she had touched him and how she had been instantly healed. Then he said to her, "Daughter, your faith has healed you. Go in peace."
—LUKE 8:44-48

Have you ever desired something, but didn't want to bother Jesus with it? What did you do?

At times we hesitate to come to God about a matter, as if He did not already know our needs. Teens may believe that something they are struggling with is too minor for God to care about or so serious that God will condemn them. They need our reassurance that they can come to their heavenly Father for even the smallest need and even the most serious sin and find mercy, healing, and forgiveness.

• • • • • • • • • • •

"Faith is like radar that sees through the fog—the reality of things at a distance that the human eye cannot see."
—CORRIE TEN BOOM, FROM *HEROES OF THE FAITH*

PRAYER: Lord, draw ___ to You in times of trouble, and enable (him/her) to believe that nothing is impossible for You to do. In Jesus' name, amen.

DAY
7

Jesus called in a loud voice, "Lazarus, come out!" The dead man came out, his hands and feet wrapped with strips of linen, and a cloth around his face. Jesus said to them, "Take off the grave clothes and let him go." Therefore many of the Jews who had come to visit Mary, and had seen what Jesus did put their faith in him.
—JOHN 11:40-45

What miracle would make your faith stronger? Without this miracle, how strong is your faith?

Miracles still happen today. Belief in them is what is lacking. If we have faith in the Source of power behind the miracles we read about in the Bible, we will see them all around us.

• • • • • • • • • • •

"Faith is a living, daring confidence in God's grace,
so sure and certain that a man could stake
his life on it a thousand times."
—MARTIN LUTHER, FROM *HEROES OF THE FAITH*

Prayer: Lord, let ___ see Your power and have
unconditional faith in You. Help (him/her)
to know when something is of You and not
the natural forces of man or nature, and
teach (him/her) to give You the glory.
In Jesus' name, amen.

Week 36
REWARD

> "I will grant peace in the land, and you will lie down and no one will make you afraid. I will remove savage beasts from the land, and the sword will not pass through your country."
> —LEVITICUS 26:6

Would the rewards mentioned in this verse satisfy you?

The rewards of this world cannot compare with those God gives us. Teens can lose sight of this when their peers seem to have so much. The scriptures are very definite about the rewards God has prepared for those who love and obey Him. Familiarity with God's promises will help teens to keep their eyes on the prize of the high calling of God.

• • • • • • • • • • •

> *"Even when we cannot see the why and the wherefore of God's dealings, we know that there is love in and behind them, and so we can rejoice always."*
> —J. I. PACKER, FROM *DAILY DEVOTIONS*

PRAYER: Lord, give ___ the courage to follow Your call so that (he/she) will receive your reward. In Jesus' name, amen.

DAY 2

*So if you faithfully obey the commands
I am giving you today—to love the LORD
your God and to serve him with all your heart
and with all your soul—then . . .
you will eat and be satisfied.*
—DEUTERONOMY 11:13, 15B

Do you really believe that God will provide all your needs if you faithfully obey His commands?

When we face illness, the loss of a job, or other crisis, and money is tight, it's hard to cling to the faith that no matter what, God will provide for all our needs. Teens are more aware than we think of the hardships their family struggles with, and anxiety can seriously impact their studies and relationships with others. When going through difficulty, do you remember to reassure your teen often that God can be counted on to make sure you eat and are satisfied?

• • • • • • • • • • •

*"Character is the ability to carry out a good resolution
long after the excitement of the moment has passed."*
—CAVETT ROBERT, FROM *THINKEXIST*

PRAYER: Lord, let ___ not give up in following
Your commandments. Let (him/her) serve You
in full confidence that You will supply every need.
In Jesus' name, amen.

DAY 3

*Learn to do right! Seek justice, encourage the
oppressed. Defend the cause of the fatherless,
plead the case of the widow. "Come now, let us
reason together," says the Lord. "Though your sins
are like scarlet, they shall be as white as snow; though
they are red as crimson, they shall be like wool."*
—ISAIAH 1:17-18

What kind of behavior does God demand of His followers? What reward is given to those who obey?

God calls those who follow Him to be holy as He is holy. Teens often are more passionate than adults in demanding justice for the poor and oppressed. Encourage them to put this natural idealism to work by using their energy and talents to make their world a better place for all.

• • • • • • • • • • •

"Today, see if you can stretch your heart and expand your love so that it touches not only those to whom you can give it easily, but also those who need it so much."
—DAPHNE ROSE KINGMA, FROM *HEART QUOTES*

PRAYER: Lord, cause ___ to desire to do what is right, to seek justice and defend those who are oppressed. Cleanse (him/her) of sin until (he/she) is as white as snow. In Jesus' name, amen.

DAY
4

He tends his flock like a shepherd: He gathers the lambs in his arms and carries them close to his heart; he gently leads those that have young.
—ISAIAH 40:11

Why do you think the Bible often pictures Jesus as our Shepherd and us as His sheep?

Sheep are wayward creatures. They need a shepherd to lead them so they don't wander astray and fall into danger. What a vivid portrayal of human beings in relation to God! Even though we don't deserve it, God gently cares for us. Young people particularly relate to the image of a lamb in the arms of the loving Shepherd. Picturing Jesus to them this way will give them confidence to run back to Him when they have wandered astray.

• • • • • • • • • • •

"His design defines your destiny."
—MAX LUCADO, FROM *CURE FOR THE COMMON LIFE*

PRAYER: Lord, let ____ always remember that You are
the good Shepherd and that You carry (him/her)
close to Your heart. In Jesus' name, amen.

DAY
5

*What good will it be for a man if he gains
the whole world, yet forfeits his soul? Or what
can a man give in exchange for his soul? For the
Son of Man is going to come in his Father's glory
with his angels, and then he will reward each
person according to what he has done.*
—MATTHEW 16:26-27

What are your goals in life right now and what reward do you expect if you reach those goals?

If our goals are God goals, we can't fail, but if we strive only for the things of this world, we will end up forfeiting our soul. Teens can be as vulnerable as adults to making idols out of material things when they put fitting in with their peers above serving God. We need to remind them and ourselves often that God will reward each of us according to what we have done, and that the things of this world have no eternal value.

• • • • • • • • • • •

"The goal of much that is written about life management is to enable us to do more in less time. But is this necessarily a desirable goal? Perhaps we need to get less done, but the right things."
—JEAN FLEMING, FROM *365 DAY BRIGHTENERS TO WARM YOUR HOME*

PRAYER: Lord, let ____ resist the devil and his
cunning ways. Show Yourself to ____ in times
when (he/she) is weak and needs Your guidance.
In Jesus' name, amen.

DAY 6

"So the last will be first, and the first will be last."
—MATTHEW 20:16

How do you see this as a good thing?

It is our human nature to want to be first. In our society we're taught to compete with others for first place from the time we're small. But Jesus taught that among God's people whoever wishes to be first must be a servant. Instead of teaching our teens to strive for the temporary adulation the world glories in, let us teach them that by serving others they will receive an eternal reward.

• • • • • • • • • • •

"The biggest reward for a thing well done is to have done it."
—VOLTAIRE, FROM *LEAD AMERICA*

> PRAYER: Lord, give ___ a spirit of service. Clothe (him/her) with compassion, kindness, humility and gentleness so (he/she) may receive Your reward.
> In Jesus' name, amen.

DAY 7

"Behold, I am coming soon! My reward is with me, and I will give to everyone according to what he has done."
—REVELATION 22:12

Why do you try to be good? What would cause you not to be good?

The desire for the splendor we read about in the Bible that Jesus promises we will share with God one day encourages us to keep reaching for the goal. Let us never grow weary in reminding our teens that Jesus is coming again to take his people back to heaven with him, and that He will reward them for all they have done in serving Him.

• • • • • • • • • • •

*"He who does not live in some degree for others,
hardly lives for himself."*
—MICHEL DE MONTAIGNE, FROM *PATCHES OF GODLIGHT*

PRAYER: Lord, help ___ to remember the promises
Christ made to those who are obedient to Him.
Give (him/her) the wisdom to always choose
Your path. In Jesus' name, amen.

DAY 1

A gentle answer turns away wrath,
but a harsh word stirs up anger.
—PROVERBS 15:1

Who do you tend to speak harshly to most often? Who do you tend to speak gently to most often? Why is that?

We often speak the most harshly to those we care about the most. When we speak hastily in anger to our teens, we stir up their anger and resentment in response. If we want to keep peace in our families, we need to learn to control our own tempers first. By correcting our teens with gentle words and appropriate discipline, we'll help them learn to control their temper and treat others with patience as well.

• • • • • • • • • • •

"We should constantly use the most common, little, easy words
(so they are pure and proper) which our language affords."
—JOHN WESLEY, FROM *HEROES OF THE FAITH*

PRAYER: Lord, take away ____'s sharp tongue and make it gentle. Let (him/her) see how others respond positively to (his/her) restraint and choose to always speak with kind words. In Jesus' name, amen.

DAY
2

Do everything without complaining or arguing.
—PHILIPPIANS 2:14

Are you able to do everything without complaining or arguing?

Just think what a utopia the world would be if everyone chose to live according to this verse. Unfortunately, it's human nature to grumble and argue, just as the children of Israel did while they wandered in the desert. An attitude of complaining and disputing makes it impossible to praise God, and the reverse is true too. By reminding our teens to continually praise God and by living that example for them, we'll hear a lot less grumbling and arguing in our families!

• • • • • • • • • •

"Whether we preach, or pray, or write, or print, or trade, or travel, take care of children, or administer the government of the state, or whatever we do, our whole life and influence should be permeated with this power."
—CHARLES FINNEY, FROM *HEROES OF THE FAITH*

PRAYER: Lord, help me to have an attitude of praise and thankgiving in everything and so be an example to ___ to do likewise. In Jesus' name, amen.

DAY
3

And we urge you, brothers, warn those who are idle, encourage the timid, help the weak, be patient with everyone.
—1 THESSALONIANS 5:14

Does this verse make meekness sound like weakness?

We tend to equate meekness with being weak, but the Bible provides a very different picture. Jesus is described as being meek, but He always acted with authority, boldness, and power. Reminding our teens that we are called not only to be patient with everyone, but also to warn the idle, encourage the timid, and help those who are weak will give them a better understanding of what true meekness involves.

• • • • • • • • • •

*The salvation of this human world lies nowhere else
than in the human heart, in the human power to reflect,
in human meekness and human responsibility.*
—VACLAV HAVEL, FROM *THINKEXIST QUOTES*

PRAYER: Lord, help ___ to have the attitude
of meekness that comes from You. Help (him/her)
to reach out to others with authority, boldness,
and power. In Jesus' name, amen.

**DAY
4**

*Remind the people to be subject to rulers and
authorities, to be obedient, to be ready to do whatever
is good, to slander no one, to be peaceable and considerate, and to show true humility toward all men.*
—TITUS 3:2

**How do you respond to people who behave according to this
verse? How do you respond to those who act the opposite?**

Our culture encourages us to fight for first place, contend
with others, and do whatever is pleasing in our own eyes.
It's difficult for teens to develop an attitude of meekness when
being peaceable and considerate can cause peers to disrespect
them. Focusing on God's rewards instead of on those of the
world can help them keep their attitudes where they ought to be.

• • • • • • • • • •

*"I seem to have been led little by little, toward my work;
and I believe that the same fact will appear in the life
of anyone who will cultivate such powers as God has
given him, and then go on, bravely, quietly, but persistently,
doing such work as comes to his hands."*
—FANNY CROSBY, FROM *HEROES OF THE FAITH*

PRAYER: Lord, teach ___ what true meekness is toward others, and help (him/her) to see the rewards of treating others with respect. In Jesus' name, amen.

My dear brothers, take note of this:
Everyone should be quick to listen,
slow to speak and slow to become angry.
—JAMES 1:19

Do you know someone who is a good model for this verse? Do you ever try to consciously be like that person?

Think of the grief we'd avoid if we took the advice to listen ten times as much as we speak! If you think about it, those who follow this verse are more likely to be the ones we turn to when we need wise counsel. If our teens learned to listen and only give their opinion when asked, they would discover that their input is sought a lot more often.

• • • • • • • • • • •

"The world does not understand theology or dogma,
but it understands love and sympathy."
—DWIGHT L. MOODY, FROM *HEROES OF THE FAITH*

PRAYER: Lord, give ___ a humble spirit and a contrite heart. Show (him/her) the blessings these traits bring and how it helps others. In Jesus' name, amen.

Who is wise and understanding among you? Let him show it by his good life, by deeds done in the humility that comes from wisdom.
—JAMES 3:13

What does wisdom result in?

Teens can be tempted to overestimate their understanding and ability, and consequently develop an arrogant attitude. If they are wise, they will heed the advice of those who have more knowledge and wisdom than they do. If not, they may learn humility by suffering the consequences of their own mistakes and failures.

• • • • • • • • • • •

"Those who make religion consistent altogether and good works, overlook the fact that works themselves are not acceptable to God and must they proceed with faith. For without faith it is impossible to please him, and those who make religion consistent altogether in faith overlook the fact that true faith always works by love, and invariably produces the works of love."
—CHARLES FINNEY, FROM *HEROES OF THE FAITH*

PRAYER: Lord, I pray that ___ will listen to those who are older and more experienced and will learn the humility that comes from wisdom. In Jesus' name, amen.

DAY 7

When they hurled their insults at him, he did not retaliate; when he suffered, he made no threats. Instead, he entrusted himself to him who judges justly.
—1 PETER 2:23

How did Jesus demonstrate true meekness when He was insulted and treated cruelly?

The teenage years can be the hardest when it comes to developing healthy self-esteem. Overt bullying and all kinds of pressure from peers to conform take a toll on even the most grounded teen. As parents, we need to help our children understand that fighting back with the same weapons only makes things worse in the long run. Instead, we are called to follow Christ's example in entrusting ourselves to the only just Judge.

• • • • • • • • • • •

Poor, weak, and worthless though I am,
I have a rich almighty friend;
Jesus, the Saviour, is His Name;
He freely loves, and without end.

He ransomed me from hell with blood,
And by His pow'r my foes controlled;
He found me wand'ring far from God,
And brought me to His chosen fold.
—JOHN NEWTON, FROM *HEROES OF THE FAITH*

PRAYER: Lord, remind ___ that all sufficiency is in You, that through Your blood we can walk before You blameless, that our past is behind us and all is forgiven. Help (him/her) to remember that You are the just Judge and to trust You to defend (him/her) in times of trouble. In Jesus' name, amen.

Week 38
COMFORT

DAY 1

For we do not have a high priest who is unable to sympathize with our weaknesses, but we have one who has been tempted in every way, just as we are— yet was without sin. Let us then approach the throne of grace with confidence, so that we may receive mercy and find grace to help us in our time of need.
—HEBREWS 4:15-16

When you picture Jesus in your mind, do you think of Him as the "perfect God," or do you sometimes picture Him as a human like yourself, who had all the temptations and feelings (good and bad) that you have? How do the two pictures make you feel different?

We can never measure up to God's standard, but He sees us through the lens of Jesus' sacrifice on the cross. As our high priest, Jesus intercedes for us, becoming the bridge between sinful humans and a holy God. By choosing to daily walk with Jesus, our teens will develop the confidence to approach the throne of grace in times of need, where they will find comfort in God's mercy and grace.

• • • • • • • • • • •

"Joy is love exalted: peace is love and repose: long-suffering is love enduring; gentleness is

225

love in society; goodness is love in action;
faith is love on the battlefield; meekness is
love in school; and temperance is love in training."
—DWIGHT L. MOODY, FROM *HEROES OF THE FAITH*

PRAYER: Lord, let ___ experience Your deliverance
and know that You take away all fears and troubles.
Give him/her) confidence to approach Your throne
in every time of need. In Jesus' name, amen.

DAY 2	*Neither height nor depth, nor anything else in all creation, will be able to separate us from the love of God that is Christ Jesus our LORD.* —ROMANS 8:39

What is able to separate us from God's love?

Think about how safe you are when you dwell in God's unconditional love. There is no greater comfort to be found than the certainty that nothing can separate us from God's love and care because of Jesus' sacrifice, not because of anything we have done or will ever have to do. When their peers turn their backs and ridicule them, our teens can find tremendous comfort in this unfailing assurance.

•••••••••••

"A child of God should be a visible Beatitude,
for joy and happiness, and a living Doxology,
for gratitude and adoration."
—CHARLES H. SPURGEON, FROM *HEROES OF THE FAITH*

PRAYER: Lord, help ___ to live in the assurance that
nothing can ever separate (him/her) from Your love
through Jesus. In Jesus' name, amen.

DAY 3

The LORD is good, a refuge in times of trouble.
He cares for those who trust in him.
—NAHUM 1:7

When you experience trouble, to whom or what do you turn first?

Teens need to learn what is lasting and what is fleeting. Because they have so little experience, it's hard for them to understand that earthly relationships and the things they can see and touch are only temporary and can only give temporary comfort. When times of trouble come, friends may fail them, but God never will. Encourage your teen to turn to God, who is the only unfailing refuge.

• • • • • • • • • • •

Ah! dearest Jesus, holy Child,
Make thee a bed, soft, undefiled,
Within my heart, that it may be
A quiet chamber kept for Thee.
—MARTIN LUTHER, FROM *HEROES OF THE FAITH*

PRAYER: Lord, seek out and be a refuge to ___ in times of trouble, as the good shepherd looks after his flock. In Jesus' name, amen.

DAY 4

Do not be afraid; you will not suffer shame.
Do not fear disgrace; you will not be humiliated.
You will forget the shame of your youth and
remember no more the reproach of your widowhood.
—ISAIAH 54:4

If you have ever suffered shame and been humiliated, what does this promise mean to you?

Shame can be a good thing if it helps us to learn from mistakes and make the right decision next time. Guilt can keep teens on the right path if it makes them stop and rethink their actions.

When we repent of our sins, God covers over our shame. We need to follow His example by forgiving our teens' errors and letting them begin anew.

• • • • • • • • • • •

"God's guidance is even more important than common sense. . . . I can declare that the deepest darkness is outshone by the light of Jesus."
—CORRIE TEN BOOM, FROM *HEROES OF THE FAITH*

PRAYER: Lord, when ___ sins, allow shame and guilt to do a good work by causing (him/her) to repent, seek Your forgiveness, and start over. In Jesus' name, amen.

DAY
5

You will surely forget your trouble, recalling it only as waters gone by.
—JOB 11:16

How easy is it for you to forget the troubles you experience? What does this verse mean to you?

When teens are going through times of deep trouble, it can be very hard for them to claim the promise of this verse. They may become vulnerable to substance abuse, harmful behaviors like cutting or eating disorders, isolation, or even suicide. Be aware of the troubles your teen is dealing with and assure him or her often that as they trust in Him, God will cause their troubles to be just like the water that flows downstream, never to be seen again.

• • • • • • • • • • •

"The happiness for which our souls ache is one undisturbed by success or failure, one which will root deeply inside us and give us inward relaxation, peace, and contentment, no matter what the surface problems may be. That kind of happiness stands in need of no outward stimulus."
—BILLY GRAHAM, FROM *HEROES OF THE FAITH*

PRAYER: Lord, let ___ return to You after times of weeping and mourning, and refresh (his/her) spirit once more. In Jesus' name, amen.

He comforts us when we are in trouble, so that we can share that same comfort with others.
— 2 CORINTHIANS 1:4

Who do you go to for comfort when you are in trouble—the Lord or a person?

Thinking of who their stronghold is should give your teen great assurance. As they learn that the difficult situations they go through enable them to comfort and encourage others in their time of trial, they will find strength to endure.

• • • • • • • • • •

God's greatness flow around our incompleteness; Round our restlessness, his rest."
—ELIZABETH BARRETT BROWNING, FROM *PATCHES OF GODLIGHT*

PRAYER: Lord, keep ___ safely in Your arms during times when (his/her) foot slips, and hold (him/her) in Your mercy. Give (him/her) wisdom not to fall into danger. And even when bad things happen around ___ let no harm come to (him/her). In Jesus' name, amen.

Even though I walk through the valley of the shadow of death, I will fear no evil, for you are with me; your rod and your staff, they comfort me.
—PSALM 23:4

When you picture Jesus with a rod and staff, what would he be doing? How is this a comforting image?

A rod is used for correction and discipline. A shepherd uses his staff to guide his sheep along the right path and to pull them to safety when they stray or get hurt. What beautiful imagery of God's constant care for us! Strive to provide the same loving discipline and guidance for your teen, even when he or she is disobedient and goes astray.

• • • • • • • • • • •

"The purpose of Christianity is not to avoid difficulty,
but to produce a character adequate to meet it when it comes.
It does not make life easy; rather it tries to make us
great enough for life.
—JAMES L. CHRISTIANSEN, FROM *WORD PRESS*

PRAYER: Lord, guide ___ with Your rod and staff when (he/she) wanders from Your path. Always bring (him/her) back to You.
In Jesus' name, amen.

Week 39
FAITH

DAY
1

*It is better to take refuge in the LORD
than to trust in man.*
—PSALM 118:8

**We know it is better to trust in the Lord than in people, but
when you have problems, who do you go first?**

We know the Lord is our refuge, yet we continue to trust
ourselves to the hands of man. We could save ourselves a
lot of grief if we could learn to start with Him and finish with
our Christian friends.

• • • • • • • • • • • •

*"Life with Christ is endless love;
without Him it is a loveless end."*
—BILLY GRAHAM, FROM *HEROES OF THE FAITH*

PRAYER: Lord, let ___ stay clear of the wicked
and find light in You. Let (him/her) meditate
on You day and night. Help us to call
on You first in times of trouble.
In Jesus' name, amen.

DAY
2

Trust in the LORD with all your heart and lean not on your own understanding.
—PROVERBS 3:5

Who do you trust and depend on more: yourself or God? Can you trust in the Lord and still take responsibility for yourself? How do you do that?

There is much to tempt and lead teens away from the Word. Experience is the best teacher, but it is hard for a parent to watch teens make the wrong choices and struggle as a consequence. We as parents also need to trust in the Lord when our teen is learning, as we learn along with our teen.

• • • • • • • • • • •

"If all things are possible with God, then all things are possible to him who believes in Him."
—CORRIE TEN BOOM, FROM *HEROES OF THE FAITH*

PRAYER: Lord, show ____ that only fools refuse You. Let (him/her) see that the ways of the wicked result in a poor outcome. In turn let (him/her) see that following You leads to great reward.
In Jesus' name, amen.

DAY
3

Therefore, since we have been justified through faith, we have peace with God through our LORD Jesus Christ.
—ROMANS 5:1

How strong is your faith? Does it fluctuate according to the challenges you face?

Teens often subtly condemn themselves when they are not walking with Christ. Feelings of guilt and unworthiness can push them even farther from God. Remind your teen often of His forever forgiveness and gently encourage him or her to return to God's path if he or she strays.

• • • • • • • • • •

"After another quiet interlude, I said, Lord,
I think you have all of me."
—JILL BRISCOE, FROM *GOD'S FRONT DOOR*

PRAYER: Lord, let ___ walk in Your spirit with a sense
of peace and an increasing hunger for You. Help
(him/her) to hold fast to You and not stray due to
feeling unworthy but to come to You for Your
never-ending mercy. In Jesus' name, amen.

DAY
4

For we also have had the gospel preached to us,
just as they did; but the message they heard was
of no value to them, because those who heard
did not combine it with faith.
—HEBREWS 4:2

Do you know people who have lots of information about the
Bible and religion but have no true faith in God? Do you feel
better about your "knowledge about God" or your "faith in
God"?

Teens must absolutely know that to make good choices is easier
when walking with God. It is a lifelong challenge to follow His
ways and feel His presence. But when they do walk with Him and
seek His face, they will find nothing else that can take its place.

• • • • • • • • • •

"When thou prayest, rather let thy heart be without words,
than thy words without a heart."
—JOHN BUNYAN, FROM *HEROES OF THE FAITH*

PRAYER: Lord, do not let ___ be hindered from
hearing Your voice. Let (him/her) listen with open
ears and a steadfast heart. Help (him/her) to be
obedient to Your guidance in (his/her) life.
In Jesus' name, amen.

DAY 5

*Now faith is being sure of what we hope for
and certain of what we do not see.*
—HEBREWS 11:1

How is the faith we have in a person different from the faith we have in God?

It's always tempting to place our faith in something that doesn't really take faith to believe. True faith is believing in something we can't see. Teens often don't understand that God sees them as holy and good regardless of their actions and feelings. He is the Almighty, and if anyone here on earth has abilities our teen admires, they come from Him, not of themselves.

• • • • • • • • • • •

> *"I believe in Christianity as I believe that the sun
> has risen; not only because I see it, but because
> by it I see everything else."*
> —C. S. LEWIS, FROM *HEROES OF THE FAITH*

PRAYER: Lord, reveal to ___ Your Spirit and rule over (his/her) heart. Don't let (him/her) be deceived by humans who claim to have all knowledge and power. Help (him/her) to discern those who are called by You and those who are not.
In Jesus' name, amen.

DAY 6

*For everyone born of God overcomes the world.
This is the victory that has overcome the world,
even our faith.*
—1 JOHN 5:4

This is a tremendous promise! If you are "born of God," how does this promise affect how you feel about your faith?

When we remember that we are born again, we recognize God's mercy and grace. As teens strive to do everything with a clean heart and mind, they will gain confidence that in God they have truly overcome the world.

• • • • • • • • • •

*"Christianity is not a theory or speculation, but a life;
not a philosophy of life, but a life and a living process."*
—SAMUEL TAYLOR COLERIDGE, FROM *WISDOM QUOTES*

> PRAYER: Lord, let ___ see the results of (his/her)
> efforts to spread the Word. Strengthen (him/her)
> in the faith that overcomes the world.
> In Jesus' name, amen.

DAY 7

*I have fought the good fight, I have finished
the race, I have kept the faith.*
— TIMOTHY 4:7

**Do you think you could survive the trials of this life without
faith?**

The race is long and hard, impossible to finish without faith.
Build up your teen so he or she can fight the good fight and
stay the course. Make his or her journey fruitful by pointing out
the good he or she does while living a life for Him.

• • • • • • • • • •

*"All who call on God in true faith, earnestly
from the heart, will certainly be heard, and will receive
what they have asked and desired."*
—MARTIN LUTHER, FROM *HEROES OF THE FAITH*

> PRAYER: Lord, strengthen ___'s heart to endure the
> race and overcome worldly trials. Help (him/her)
> never to forget what (his/her) goal is and the victory
> that lies ahead. In Jesus' name, amen.

Week 40
ZEAL

DAY
1

*"Arise, shine, for your light has come,
and the glory of the* LORD *rises upon you.*
—ISAIAH 60:1

Does this describe how you get up in the morning? If you made it a practice every morning when you first get up to think that "the glory of the Lord rises upon you" how do you think your day might go differently than usual?

Knowing that their attitude is a choice may make a difference in teens' demeanor and decisions. When they put God first before self, they will discover that power becomes available to them to change the way they proceed with their day.

• • • • • • • • • • • •

*"We should live our lives as though Christ
were coming this afternoon."*
—JIMMY CARTER, FROM *NOTEABLE QUOTES*

PRAYER: Lord, fill ___ with joy and sustain (him/her)
with a strong heart. Let (him/her) see Your glory
and power and take comfort in knowing that You
can protect (him/her) in all situations.
In Jesus' name, amen.

*Those who are wise will shine like the brightness
of the heavens, and those who lead many
to righteousness, like the stars for ever and ever.*
—DANIEL 12:3

**Do you know anyone who fits this description? What is your
opinion of this person? Are you like him or her? Would you
like to be?**

As parents, we need to praise our teens' efforts to make wise
choices and become a shining example to others even when
they sometimes make mistakes. Through tactful advice and
encouragement, we can empower them to share their faith with
their peers when the opportunity arises.

• • • • • • • • • • •

"The stars rule men, but God rules the stars."
—CHRISTOPH CELLARIUS, FROM *WORLD OF QUOTES*

PRAYER: Lord, help ___ to be wise and strong in
leading others to Your fold. Let (him/her) make a
practice of memorizing Bible verses and give
(him/her) the ability to remember them when
(he/she) needs the words to come.
In Jesus' name, amen.

*But he replied, "LORD, I am ready to go
with you to prison and to death."*
—LUKE 22:33

**What hardship are you ready to go through with the Lord?
What would you not want to face, even with the Lord?**

It's important to prepare teens to deal with hardships because
they will inevitably come. Teaching them to lean on God even
during good times instead of on the comforts of the world is one
of the best ways to ensure they'll stand strong when they go
through times of trial.

• • • • • • • • • • •

"This world is God's workshop for making men in."
—HENRY WARD BEECHER, FROM *GOD QUOTES AND SAYINGS*

PRAYER: Lord, give ___ strength to endure the trials
You allow (him/her) to experience. Give ___ the
assurance that You have a plan for (him/her) and will
prosper (him/her) through the refining process.
In Jesus' name, amen.

DAY 4

Never be lacking in zeal, but keep your spiritual fervor, serving the LORD.
—ROMANS 12:11

Have you ever lost your zeal for serving the Lord? Why and how did you get it back—if you did?

There will be peaks and valleys for teens, even when they serve God. We must be prepared for times when they doubt and question their faith. Relying on scripture gives your answers spiritual power and teaches them where to go with their questions.

• • • • • • • • • • •

"A true love to God must begin with a delight in his holiness."
—JONATHAN EDWARDS, FROM *HEROES OF THE FAITH*

PRAYER: Lord, let ___ reverence and follow
You instead of the urgings of (his/her) own flesh.
Give (him/her) the confidence to trust that You
are the way, the truth, and the life.
In Jesus' name, amen.

DAY
5

*It is fine to be zealous, provided the purpose is good,
and to be so always and not just when I am with you.*
—GALATIANS 4:18

**Are you more "zealous" when you are around other Christians?
If so, why?**

Remind your teen that zeal for Christ comes from the heart.
Putting on a show to impress others will have the opposite
effect. By living out their love for the Lord in a humble way, they
will influence others to desire the faith they have.

• • • • • • • • • •

*"Walk boldly and wisely. . . . There is a hand above
that will help you on."*
—PHILIP JAMES BAILEY, FROM *FAMOUS QUOTES AND AUTHORS*

PRAYER: Lord, let ___ be honest in (his/her) walk
with You and be true to (himself or herself)
with no deception. Help (him/her) to think
through actions so (he/she) will have no regrets
and will honor You. In Jesus' name, amen.

DAY
6

*Let us not become weary in doing good,
for at the proper time we will reap a harvest
if we do not give up.*
—GALATIANS 6:9

**What in your life right now are you spending time and energy
on without seeing rewards? How do you feel about "doing
good for good's sake" and never receiving a reward for it?**

Learning to work without receiving the rewards of our labor
on this earth is hard even for adults. The assurance that they
will reap a harvest, if they don't become weary in doing good,
will help teens to persevere when the results aren't apparent.

• • • • • • • • • •

"God is a good worker, but loves to be helped."
—BASQUE PROVERB, FROM *PATCHES OF GODLIGHT*

PRAYER: Lord, give ___ only what (he/she) can bear
and be by (his/her) side as (he/she) lives out Your
calling. Let (him/her) shine on as (he/she)
continues to do good for all to see.
In Jesus' name, amen.

DAY 7

*One thing I do: Forgetting what is behind
and straining toward what is ahead, I press on
toward the goal to win the prize for which God
has called me heavenward in Christ Jesus.*
—PHILIPPIANS 3:13B-14

**How could forgetting what is behind and straining toward
what is ahead help you in your everyday life? What is behind
you that you need to forget?**

Zeal enables teens to press on through obstacles and difficulties. When they truly know that God has not only forgiven
their sins but has also forgotten them, they will be freed to put
the past behind them and strain toward what is ahead.

• • • • • • • • • • •

*The Christian ideal has not been tried and found wanting.
It has been found difficult and left untried."*
—G. K. CHESTERTON, FROM *PATCHES OF GODLIGHT*

PRAYER: Lord, let ___ not hang onto what
is past, but rather to forge ahead with what
You have planned for (him/her). Help (him/her)
not to look back to sins of old but to make a new life
through faith in You. In Jesus' name, amen.

241

FRUITFUL

I will set before my eyes no vile thing. The deeds of faithless men I hate; they will not cling to me.
—PSALM 101:3

Think of something that was not good for you spiritually, that you used to really want. What caused you not to want it anymore?

Teens need to develop discernment to understand why certain things are not good for them spiritually and others are. The better they understand the reasons behind our rules, the easier it will be for them to choose what is good before becoming defiled by harmful things and behaviors and finding it is even harder to give them up once they become a habit.

• • • • • • • • • • •

"You are remembered for the rules you break."
—DOUGLAS MACARTHUR, FROM *GREAT QUOTES FROM GREAT LEADERS*

PRAYER: Lord, let ____ listen to godly counselors, be teachable, and recognize (his/her) own errors. Help (him/her) to grow from these experiences and become new in Your eyes so (he/she) in turn can help others with their spiritual growth.
In Jesus' name, amen.

243

*Discretion will protect you, and
understanding will guard you.*
—PROVERBS 2:11

**When is the last time you consciously made a choice that pro-
tected you from sin or from being hurt?**

Making note of the times when they have felt protected can
help teens during difficult times ahead. Remembering
these times will help keep them strong and ready when those
temptations come again.

• • • • • • • • • • •

*"One cannot and must not try to erase the past
merely because it does not fit the present."*
—GOLDA MEIR, FROM *WORDSKIT*

PRAYER: Lord, keep ___'s eyes on You. May (he/she)
have ears to hear Your voice. Make (him/her) ready
and willing to follow You and do Your will.
In Jesus' name, amen.

*The fruit of righteousness will be peace;
the effect of righteousness will be quietness
and confidence forever.*
—ISAIAH 32:17

**Would you describe your daily life as generally peaceful,
inwardly quiet, and confident regardless of what is going on
around you? Do you consider yourself a righteous person? Why
can you think of yourself as righteous and not be bragging?**

Knowing how to find get to that place of peace and quiet can
keep teens on the right path. Having regular alone time to
feed upon God's word and pray, and knowing the signs to look
for will keep them from drifting off the path of righteousness.

• • • • • • • • • • •

"You must pay the price if you wish to secure the blessing."
—ANDREW JACKSON, FROM *GREAT QUOTES FROM GREAT LEADERS*

PRAYER: Lord, let ___ clearly hear the call
You have for (him/her) and know that (he/she) was
created for a higher purpose. Keep (him/her) humbly
by Your side as You guide (him/her) over life's hurdles and teach (him/her) how to live a godly life.
In Jesus' name, amen.

DAY
4

Remain in me, and I will remain in you.
No branch can bear fruit by itself; it must
remain in the vine. Neither can you bear
fruit unless you remain in me.
—JOHN 15:4

Does this verse add pressure on you to "bear fruit," or does it make you feel relieved? Why?

Knowing they always have Christ with them for strength to do what they should will encourage teens. Understanding what their spiritual gifts are will help them to develop their abilities and recognize opportunities to use them.

• • • • • • • • • •

"Are you green and growing or ripe and rotting?"
—RAY KROC, FROM *EZINEARTICLES*

PRAYER: Lord, let ___ acknowledge that You
unite (his/her) heart with Yours as (he/she) walks
in Your truth. Open ___'s eyes to (his/her) spiritual
gifts and make it clear what to do with those gifts.
In Jesus' name, amen.

DAY
5

But the fruit of the Spirit is love, joy, peace, patience, kindness, goodness, faithfulness, gentleness and self-control. Against such things there is no law.
—GALATIANS 5:22–23

Which of these eight fruits is the biggest blessing for you? How would your life change if at the end of each day, you consciously thought of how you to enjoyed those fruits that day?

Continue to encourage your teen to bear good fruit. Help him or her to shower the blessings of this fruit on others, and let others see what God has given to him or her. Recognize the fruit of the spirit that your teen shows and let them know you see it.

• • • • • • • • • •

"Ability is a poor man's wealth."
—JOHN WOODEN, FROM *GREAT QUOTES FROM GREAT LEADERS*

PRAYER: Lord, deliver ___ from unfruitfulness. Let (him/her) rise up boldly and acknowledge You when bearing fruit before others. Keep (him/her) humble and kind at these times.
In Jesus' name, amen.

DAY
6

For the fruit of the light consists in all goodness, righteousness and truth.
—EPHESIANS 5:9

If you are saved and a child of God, when is it easy to be good, righteous, and truthful?

To feel free in the Spirit is uplifting and life changing. Remind your teen what that feels like and all the ways he or she is set free because of the love of Christ.

• • • • • • • • • •

"Actions are the seeds of fate deeds grow into destiny."
—HARRY S. TRUMAN, FROM *GREAT QUOTES FROM GREAT LEADERS*

> PRAYER: Lord, may ___ know the truth and let
> the truth set (him/her) free. Let (him/her) share
> the truth with others as (he/she) bears witness
> of Your never-changing love and forgiveness.
> In Jesus' name, amen.

And this is my prayer: that your love may abound more and more in knowledge and depth of insight, so that you may be able to discern what is best and may be pure and blameless until the day of Christ, filled with the fruit of righteousness that comes through Jesus Christ—to the glory and praise of God.
—PHILIPPIANS 1:9-11

Have you ever tried to be righteous without Jesus? How did it work?

We can always be good for a brief time on our own, but at some point we inevitably fail. Be an example to your teen of always turning to God when things are not going our way. Help him or her to learn not to depend on other people and things that are a temporary fix, but on what is lasting.

• • • • • • • • • • •

"I am in politics because of the conflict between good and evil, and I believe that in the end good will triumph."
—MARGARET THATCHER, FROM *GREAT QUOTES FROM GREAT LEADERS*

> PRAYER: Lord, let ___ rest in Your wisdom and might.
> Help (him/her) to see what You alone can provide as
> no other can. Help (him/her) to remember where
> true joy and peace come from and thank You.
> In Jesus' name, amen.

Week 42

PERSEVERANCE

DAY 1

Therefore, my dear brothers, stand firm. Let nothing move you. Always give yourselves fully to the work of the LORD, because you know that your labor in the LORD is not in vain.
—1 CORINTHIANS 15:58

What is most discouraging to you about doing the work of the Lord? How does this verse help you?

During times when your teen feels overwhelmed, remind him or her that what we do is for a higher purpose. It's important to encourage teens to stand firm, knowing that their labor is never in vain in the Lord.

• • • • • • • • • • •

"The purpose of human life is to serve and to show compassion and the will to help others."
—ALBERT SCHWEITZER, FROM *GOOD THOUGHTS*

PRAYER: Lord, protect ___'s mind and shield (him/her) from the enemy. Give (him/her) the strength that can only come from you.
In Jesus' name, amen.

DAY
2

Test everything. Hold on to the good.
—1 THESSALONIANS 5:21

What does it mean to test everything? How do you do that?

Teens tend to be curious and want to explore unfamiliar things. Whet your teen's curiosity about the Lord and His power. The more they seek His face, the more fully He will reveal Himself to them.

• • • • • • • • • • •

"Far better is it to dare mighty things, to win glorious triumphs even though checkered by failure, than to rank with those poor spirits who neither enjoy nor suffer much because they live in a gray twilight that knows neither victory nor defeat."
—THEODORE ROOSEVELT, FROM *GREAT QUOTES FROM GREAT LEADERS*

PRAYER: Lord, do not let the Evil One
hold ___'s mind captive. Help (him/her) to resist sin,
and cleanse (his/her) mind. Help (him/her) to
become aware of Satan's oppression and cast it away.
In Jesus' name, amen.

DAY
3

May our LORD Jesus Christ himself and God our Father, who loved us and by his grace gave us eternal encouragement and good hope, encourage your hearts and strengthen you in every good deed and word.
—2 THESSALONIANS 2:16-17

If God loves us no matter what and encourages us all the time, how do you explain the times you are discouraged?

Much learning comes from discomfort. It is hard for teens to understand that pain builds strength. But going through hard times enables God to shape and mold them to His image.

• • • • • • • • • • •

In whatever direction you turn, you will see God coming to meet you; nothing is void of Him; He himself fills all His work."
—SENECA THE YOUNGER, FROM *PATCHES OF GODLIGHT*

PRAYER: Lord, give ___ Your peace and guard (his/her) heart and mind in Christ. Let (him/her) rest in You when tired and weak, knowing You will care for (him/her) as a parent for a child.
In Jesus' name, amen.

DAY
4

Endure hardship with us like a good soldier of Christ Jesus.
—2 TIMOTHY 2:3

When you experience hardship, do you get discouraged? How can you keep a positive attitude?

We need to help our teens to fight against discouragement during times of hardship. Guide your teen in the direction of Christ. Remind him or her of how God blessed even in difficult times in the past.

• • • • • • • • • • • •

"I have learned that success is to be measured not so much by the position that one has reached in life as by the obstacles which he has had to overcome while trying to succeed."
—BOOKER T. WASHINGTON, FROM *GOOD READS*

PRAYER: Lord, let ___ claim You when negative thoughts and discouragement torment (his/her) soul. In Jesus' name, amen.

Therefore, since we are surrounded by such a great cloud of witnesses, let us throw off everything that hinders and the sin that so easily entangles, and let us run with perseverance the race marked out for us.
—HEBREWS 12:1

It seems that hardships are harder to endure when we carry sin with us. Why is it often hard to want to get rid of something that hinders and entangles us?

Sometimes we enjoy sin so much that we ignore God's help to resist temptation so we can hold onto that pleasure. Reminding our teens that they have a great cloud of witnesses cheering them on can help them to cast sin off and run their race with perseverance.

• • • • • • • • • • •

"Come what may, all bad fortune is to be conquered by endurance."
—VIRGIL, FROM *BRAINY QUOTES*

PRAYER: Lord, help ___ to resist temptation. Make (him/her) strong and let (him/her) see how much more (he/she) can bear in the strength You have blessed (him/her) with. In Jesus' name, amen.

Perseverance must finish its work so that you may be mature and complete, not lacking anything.
—JAMES 1:4

What in your life requires the most perseverance? Why do you suppose that is?

When teens learn to allow perseverance to finish its work, they will become mature and complete, not lacking in anything. As parents, we can guide them through this process in the assurance that God is with us every step of the way.

• • • • • • • • • •

*"Physical strength can never permanently
withstand the impact of spiritual force."*
—Franklin Roosevelt, from *Great Quotes from Great Leaders*

PRAYER: Lord, do not let ___ be broken down
by evil where (he/she) is weak. Take charge of
(his/her) spirit. Let (him/her) learn of Your ways
and stay on the straight and narrow path
along the journey. In Jesus' name, amen.

DAY 7

*Blessed is the man who perseveres under trial,
because when he has stood the test, he will
receive the crown of life that God has promised
those who love him.*
—James 1:12

What gives you the incentive to persevere?

It's important that teens learn to look beyond immediate gratification to the long-term gain. Reminding them that God has promised the crown of life to those who love him will help them to persevere under trial and stand the test.

• • • • • • • • • •

*"Obstacles are those frightful things you see
when you take your eyes off your goal."*
—Henry Ford, from *Great Quotes from Great Leaders*

PRAYER: Lord, help ___ to be repulsed by sin and to
reject it fully. Open (his/her) eyes to see where the
darkness lies and where (he/she) will find the light.
In Jesus' name, amen.

Week 43
PATIENCE

DAY
1

Be still before the LORD and wait patiently for him; do not fret when men succeed in their ways, when they carry out their wicked schemes.
—PSALM 37:7

What emotion comes most easily for you when you see other people "win" even though they didn't deserve it?

Winning may be something as simple as learning from an experience, even though you don't get the prize. Don't allow your teen to be deceived into believing that the evil ways of the world lead to success. Sometimes we need to allow teens to learn from experience, and when they suffer consequences, support and lift them up so they can stand strong the next time.

• • • • • • • • • • •

"The first duty of love is to listen."
—PAUL TILLICH, FROM *BRAINY QUOTE*

PRAYER: Lord, teach ___ to love and care for others. Help (him/her) to urge those who are caught up in wickedness to turn around, and to not be ashamed to witness about You.
In Jesus' name, amen.

DAY 2

*The end of a matter is better than its beginning,
and patience is better than pride.*
—ECCLESIASTES 7:8

How can this verse help you to be patient when unfair things happen?

Many things in life are not fair in a human perspective. Trusting that God is in control and being patient to let God work in His own time will lessen the frustration that comes from dwelling on 'unfairness'. It's easy to lose patience with teens when they have clearly done something wrong, especially if they aren't honest about what they did. To admit that you are wrong is difficult, especially for those who are proud. Follow through with what you know is right, but also commend your teen if he or she comes forth with the truth.

• • • • • • • • • • •

*"It makes no sense to seek your God-given strength
until you trust his."*
—MAX LUCADO, FROM *CURE FOR THE COMMON LIFE*

> PRAYER: Lord, help ___ to break through any
> hardheadedness, and bring (him/her) into balance.
> Help (him/her) to see (his/her) faults and learn to
> deal with pride. In Jesus' name, amen.

DAY 3

It is good to wait quietly for the salvation of the LORD.
—LAMENTATIONS 3:26

This is a good verse to remember when things are falling apart and you don't have any control over them. When is the last time you felt this way?

Usually we feel out of control when we are trying to control things that should be left to God. We need to do what we can and quietly trust God for the results. Remembering the goal we are working for helps us to keep our emotions in check along the way. Teens may try to act like they are doing okay in stressful situations, but it's good to know what signs to look for when times are harder than usual and they may need some extra help.

• • • • • • • • • • •

"There is nothing quite so valuable as work.
That's why it is a good idea to leave some for tomorrow."
—MARIAN DOLLIVER, FROM *PATCHES OF GODLIGHT*

PRAYER: Lord, remind ___ that salvation is nearer than when (he/she) first believed and to cast off the works of darkness, that each day we grow closer to the day of Your return, and that we need to make ready for that day. In Jesus' name, amen.

DAY 4

Be joyful in hope, patient in affliction,
faithful in prayer.
—ROMANS 12:12

It is really hard for most of us to be patient in affliction. How can hope and prayer help us with that?

Faith and hope are sometimes all we have, and they bring us closer to God than anything else. These terms complement each other to create a firm foundation when times are at their worst. We know we can go to our Father during times of affliction and learn patience to see us through with joy and hope.

• • • • • • • • • • •

"The secret of success is constancy of purpose."
—BENJAMIN DISRAELI, FROM *PATCHES OF GODLIGHT*

PRAYER: Lord, let ___ cast off the darkness and put on the armor of light. Give (him/her) the firm foundation of Your promise for tomorrow. In Jesus' name, amen.

DAY 5

Love is patient, love is kind, it does not envy, it does not boast, it is not proud.
— 1 CORINTHIANS 13:4

Think of someone you truly love. Do you find it easier to be patient and kind and not envy, or to be boastful around this person? Why do you suppose that is?

We should model the kinds of relationships we want our teens to form for themselves. Although life can get in the way and we as parents are not perfect, showing our teens examples of strong Christian love through our friendships is the best way to help them stay out of bad relationships.

• • • • • • • • • • •

"Half our life is spent trying to find something to do with the time we have rushed through life trying to save."
—WILL ROGERS, FROM *MEDITATIONS FOR PARENTS WHO DO TOO MUCH*

PRAYER: Lord, teach ____ to be warm, tender, compassionate, and loving. Help us to provide that model even when times get rough. When we do slip, help us to ask for forgiveness so (he/she) will learn to as well.
In Jesus' name, amen.

DAY 6

We remain pure. We understand completely what it means to serve God. We are patient and kind. We serve him in the power of the Holy Spirit. We serve him with true love.
—2 CORINTHIANS 6:6

Why do you need the Holy Spirit to do all of these things?

To have the Holy Spirit is like having an ally for every need. Urge your teen to take full advantage of the holy soldier who is intimately there when he or she gets lost and needs God's support.

• • • • • • • • • • •

*"Family life is an existential classroom
that lasts about eighteen years."*
—GORDON MACDONALD, FROM *365 DAY BRIGHTENERS TO WARM YOUR HOME*

> PRAYER: Lord, let ___ openly confess (his/her) errors
> and change habits of indifference. Drive (him/her) to
> care and be passionate about (his/her) relationship
> with the Father, the Son, and the Holy Spirit.
> In Jesus' name, amen.

*Being strengthened with all power according
to his glorious might so that you may have
great endurance and patience.*
—COLOSSIANS 1:11

**Do you find yourself trying harder to endure in your own
strength, or do you remember to look to God for power?**

We will always run short of endurance and patience on our
own. It's only as we look to God that we receive all power
through his glorious might. The next time your teen struggles
against obstacles, remind him or her that trusting in our own
strength won't get us through when we grow weary, but that in
God's strength we can endure and claim the victory.

• • • • • • • • • • •

*"The struggle of life is one of our greatest blessings. It makes us
patient, sensitive, and Godlike. It teaches us that although the
world is full of suffering, it is also full of the overcoming of it."*
—HELEN KELLER, FROM *BEST INSPIRATION*

> PRAYER: Lord, restore what needs to be restored in
> ___'s life and protect (him/her) from
> disappointment and apathy. Let (him/her) choose
> the good and overcome the bad.
> In Jesus' name, amen.

Week 44
PARENTS

Now you have been pleased to bless the house of your servant that it may continue forever in your sight; for you, O LORD, have blessed it, and it will be blessed forever.
—1 CHRONICLES 17:27

What do you think it means to have God bless your house?

Think of what it means to have the Lord in your home right there with you, to know your comings and goings throughout the day and night. This might encourage your teen to think before going down the wrong path.

• • • • • • • • • •

"The development of strong character must be emphasized and rewarded in the home."
—CHARLES STANLEY, FROM *365 DAY BRIGHTENERS TO WARM YOUR HOME*

> PRAYER: Lord, close the door to any negative influences that seek to encroach upon ___.
> Remind us to encourage the good behavior as well as rebuff the bad. In Jesus' name, amen.

*So the next generation would know [God's law],
even the children yet to be born, and they
in turn would tell their children.*
—PSALM 78:6

How did your parents teach you about God's law? Are you following their example? If so, is it working?

If our descendents are to know God, then we must lead our teens to Him through the Word and prayer. Knowing how to do this as a parent can be difficult, especially if we came to the Lord later in life. We need to seek out the Lord's direction.

••••••••••

*"Every material goal, even if it is met, will pass away.
But the heritage of children is timeless.
Our children are our messages to the future."*
—BILLY GRAHAM, FROM *HEROES OF THE FAITH*

PRAYER: Lord, help us to spend time together as a family, studying the Word and seeking You. Let us be the parents You want us to be, not withholding what You expect from us. In Jesus' name, amen.

*As a father has compassion on his children, so the
Lord has compassion on those who fear him.*
—PSALM 103:13

Do you have compassion for your children the way God has compassion for you?

Compassion has become a rare quality in a culture that teaches people to think about "number one." If we can keep God first before the many idols we and our teens are tempted to worship, our families will be able to stay on the straight and narrow path instead of drifting onto the the world's highway.

••••••••••

*"As we let our own light shine, we unconsciously
give other people permission to do the same."*
—NELSON MANDELA, FROM *GREAT QUOTES FROM GREAT LEADERS*

PRAYER: Lord, let ___ feel toward You the good
and righteous fear that comes from reverence.
Teach (him/her) to respect us as the ones You have
provided to care for (him/her) on this earth.
In Jesus' name, amen.

DAY 4	*Train a child in the way he should go, and when he is old he will not turn from it.* —PROVERBS 22:6

Is training a child not only teaching, but also the method used in the teaching?

Being an example for a teen is the best way to get through to him or her. We need to let our teens see our mistakes and how we deal with them. Do we go to God first or to one another to rectify the sin? What we do and what we say need to match up for our children's sake.

• • • • • • • • • • •

*"Home is the first school and first church
for young ones, where they learn what is right,
what is good, and what is kind."*
—ERNESTINE SCHUMANN-HEINK, FROM *MOTIVATE US*

PRAYER: Lord, let us fulfill the vision You have
for ___ and teach us how You want (him/her) to
grow. Help us to show (him/her) through our
relationship with You how to correct mistakes
in a way that glorifies You. In Jesus' name, amen.

Leave your orphans; I will protect their lives.
Your widows too can trust in me.
—JEREMIAH 49:11

Do you think that God has special compassion for widows and orphans? Why do you think this could be true?

We must not forget about those most in need. It's so hard for most of us—and even harder for our teens—to see others' desperate situations when we live such different lives. Our concerns become very small when we encounter those who have nothing.

• • • • • • • • • • •

"Don't miss the place to find your place and heal your hurts."
—MAX LUCADO, FROM *CURE FOR THE COMMON LIFE*

PRAYER: Lord, let ___ remember those who have less and reach out to them. Help (him/her) to grow a big heart in Your name, letting Your light shine through. In Jesus' name, amen.

Fathers, do not exasperate your children;
instead, bring them up in the training and
instruction of the LORD.
—EPHESIANS 6:4

Sometimes learning results in exasperation for the learner as well as the teacher. When might this be the bad exasperation this verse talks about, and when might it be good exasperation, which does not damage relationships?

Family relationships can become strained during difficult times, but learning from mistakes can relieve future frustration. Sometimes it just takes time to change and grow into what God wants us to be.

• • • • • • • • • • •

*"As I contemplate the kind of future I want for children,
my own and other people's, I believe we must look inward to God
for guidance and strength, and backward to draw on the values
and legacies of our families, ancestors and communities."*
—MARIAN WRIGHT EDELMAN, FROM *365 DAY BRIGHTENERS TO
WARM YOUR HOME*

PRAYER: Lord, help ___ to have good communication
with (his/her) father and to develop a relationship
of mutual respect and understanding.
In Jesus' name, amen.

DAY
7

*Endure hardship as discipline; God is
treating you as sons. For what son is not
disciplined by his father?*
—HEBREWS 12:17

When have you felt as if you were disciplined by God? Did you fight it?

For teens to know when God is disciplining them and that what they're going through has a purpose and a reason might make the process easier.

• • • • • • • • • • •

"Life isn't a matter of milestones but of moments."
—ROSE FITZGERALD KENNEDY, FROM *TASTE OF HOME*

PRAYER: Lord, guide ___, however painful it may be,
so that (he/she) can bring forth fruit. Help (him/her)
to stay strong, knowing that this experience will
bring You glory. In Jesus' name, amen.

Week 45
WORSHIP

*Within your temple, O God, we meditate
on your unfailing love.*
—PSALM 48:9

What do you do during worship time in church?

It doesn't matter how a teen worships, just that he or she is worshiping. It is biblical for us to raise hands, dance, and sing as we praise God. It is also okay to remain silent and just take it all in. God knows the heart.

• • • • • • • • • • •

*"God loves each one of us as if
there were only one of us."*
—ST. AUGUSTINE, FROM *QUOTATIONS BOOK*

PRAYER: Lord, let the joy of Your heart flow
through ___ as (he/she) worships You.
In Jesus' name, amen.

DAY
2

Ascribe to the Lord the glory due his name;
worship the Lord in the splendor of his holiness.
—PSALM 29:2

Is your image of God one of glory and splendor and holiness, or is it one of a more ordinary, human nature? Describe your image of God.

Discussing with teens how they envision God can help to define that image for them. We want our teens to see God as a personal and approachable God and also to delight in His glory and the splendor of His holiness.

• • • • • • • • • •

"There is just one way to bring up a child in the way he should go, and that is to travel that way yourself."
—ABRAHAM LINCOLN, FROM *GREAT QUOTES FROM GREAT LEADERS*

PRAYER: Lord, let ___ see Your promises, Your ways, and Your power. Let (him/her) acknowledge You in all things. In Jesus' name, amen.

DAY
3

Worship the LORD in the splendor of his holiness;
tremble before him, all the earth.
—PSALM 96:9

Why would you tremble before someone? When we tremble before God, how do you think He expects us to feel about Him?

If teens can think of someone they admire so much that they have a respectful fear of that person, it might help them to understand how much we need to revere God.

• • • • • • • • • •

Before church, we talk to God; during church, God talks to us;
after church we talk to our neighbors.
—ANONYMOUS, FROM *WISE WORD AND QUOTES*

PRAYER: Lord, let ___ feel Your holy, awesome power and feel the shield of protection that surrounds (him/her) each day. In Jesus' name, amen.

DAY 4

Exalt the LORD our God and worship at his footstool; he is holy.
—PSALM 99:5

If you were writing this verse in today's language, how would you phrase it and why?

Is there something in our culture today to which you could compare worshiping at God's footstool? If so, it could give a greater understanding of how we should exalt and worship God.

•••••••••••

"The soul at its highest is found like God, but an angel gives a closer idea of Him. That is all an angel is, an idea of God.
—MEISTER ECKHART, FROM WISE WORDS AND QUOTES

PRAYER: Lord, give ___ the favor of basking in Your presence. Strengthen (his/her) faith to move mountains. In Jesus' name, amen.

DAY 5

Worship the Lord with gladness; come before him with joyful songs.
—PSALM 100:2

Does this describe your feelings at worship, or are you more serious and somber? Which works better for you?

We should allow our teens to glorify God as creatively as is natural to them. Encourage teens to let their hands fly and to lift their voices to the Lord or to be still and meditate on the songs of praise.

•••••••••••

*"To love is to learn the song that is in their heart and
to sing it to them when they have forgotten."*
—ANONYMOUS

PRAYER: Lord, give ___ an extra measure of faith
today and feed (his/her) soul with Your glory.
In Jesus' name, amen.

DAY 6	*Then they cried out to the LORD in their trouble, and he delivered them from their distress.* —PSALM 107:6

When have you cried out to the Lord in the midst of trouble? How did He deliver you?

If teens can think beyond the immediate problem and separate emotions from facts, they will usually find a reasonable solution. But that can be hard for teens dealing with hormones and mood swings. Correct timing can be crucial when discussing the issues involved.

• • • • • • • • • •

*"When we call on Him, God bends down His ear to listen,
as a father bends down to listen to a little child."*
—KITTY TREVYLYN, FROM THE *DIARY OF KITTY TREVYLYN*

PRAYER: Lord, let ___ seek You, rely on You, be led by
You, and acknowledge You in all things.
In Jesus' name, amen.

DAY 7	*Who will not fear you, O LORD, and bring glory to your name? For you alone are holy. All nations will come and worship before you, for your righteous acts have been revealed.* —REVELATION 15:4

In the world today, does it seem as if "all nations will come and worship before God"? What could make that happen in your world?

Help teens to think into the future. What it will be like ten, twenty, or more years from now? Prepare them for the changes that are likely to come. Especially prepare them to become disciples of Jesus and to follow the path He has laid out for them to tread.

• • • • • • • • • • •

*"It becomes us humbly to approach the throne
of Almighty God, with gratitude and praise
for the wonders which his goodness has wrought."*
—U.S. CONGRESS 1779 THANKSGIVING PROCLAMATION, FROM *PILGRIM HALL*

PRAYER: Lord, give ___ Your vision and help
(him/her) to know that everything is possible
through You. Help ___ to find (his/her) part
in doing Your will in the world.
In Jesus' name, amen.

Week 46

GOLDEN RULE

DAY 1

"Do to others what you would have them do to you."
—Matthew 7:12

When you read this, what is your first thought—that others should treat your better, or that you should treat other people better? What does that tell you about yourself?

To follow the Golden Rule is to be most Christ-like. Although in our own power we can't live as this verse commands, the Holy Spirit empowers us to love others even as Christ loved in dying for us on the cross. Remind your teen to seek this holy power when dealing with difficult people.

• • • • • • • • • •

"In life sometimes we have to live by what other people want rather than what we ourselves want, and we just have to accept it."
—Kevin Burns, from *Patches of Godlight*

PRAYER: Lord, let ___ always be active in service for You, treating others as You would have us to. In Jesus' name, amen.

DAY 2

But a Samaritan, as he traveled, came where the man was; and when he saw him, he took pity on him.
—LUKE 10:33

If you see a stranger in trouble, what is your first thought: to get away before you get involved in something that might hurt you or to go and help without thinking of the consequences?

Teens who have the confidence to help others when needed are to be admired, especially if the one in trouble isn't accepted by their peers, just as the Samaritan wasn't accepted in the time of Christ. Remind your teens that they never know when they may be the one who needs a favor.

• • • • • • • • • •

"Heroes and cowards have the same obstacles and fears, they just look at them differently."
—L. S., AGE 13

PRAYER: Lord, let ____ feel the compassion
and the desire to help others that only You can
instill into our hearts. In Jesus' name, amen.

DAY 3

Accept one another, then, just as Christ accepted you, in order to bring praise to God.
—ROMANS 15:7

We know that Christ accepted all kinds of people. What kinds of people are easy for you to accept, and what kinds are really hard for you to accept?

If we accept all God's people, we bring praise to God. This is hard for teens who worry about fitting in with their peer group, as so many do. Reminding teens of times when they were the one left out may help to soften their hearts.

• • • • • • • • • •

"If you become a burning light of justice and peace in the world, then really you will be true to what the founders of this country stood for. God bless you!"
—MOTHER TERESA, FROM *HEROES OF THE FAITH*

PRAYER: Lord, help ____ to understand the needs of others and to look at them with Your eyes by Your standards. In Jesus' name, amen.

DAY
4

Praise be to the God and Father of our LORD Jesus Christ, the Father of compassion and the God of all comfort, who comforts us in all our troubles, so that we can comfort those in any trouble with the comfort we ourselves have received from God.
—2 CORINTHIANS 1:34

Do you find it difficult to listen to a friend's troubles when you are struggling with problems of your own?

By seeking the Lord's guidance, teens can become the kind of friend they hope to be and to have. As they reflect on times when they were down and needed a lift, they will develop empathy for others when they need it.

• • • • • • • • • • •

"Love is like a roller coaster ride. Even through all the ups and downs, twists and turns, screams and shouts, I am very glad I got on."
—BRITTANY O., AGE 19

PRAYER: Lord, help ____ to find (his/her) identity in You and see (his/her) true self-worth. Lead (him/her) to reach out to others in Your love. In Jesus' name, amen.

*Carry each other's burdens, and in this way
you will fulfill the law of Christ.*
—GALATIANS 6:2

Are you a better "carrier of other's burdens," or are you better at giving others the opportunity to carry your burdens?

The give and take of friendship provides the opportunity to minister to one another as we carry another's burdens, and then relinqish our burdens to others. Teens need to understand this balance so they don't become either overwhelmed or selfish.

• • • • • • • • • •

*A little girl arrived home late from school. Her mother
asked her why. "I had to help another girl. She was in trouble,"
replied the daughter. "What did you do to help her?"
the mother asked. "Oh, I sat down and helped her cry."*
—ANONYMOUS

PRAYER: Lord, let ___ see the unique qualities
in everyone and be able to appreciate them
as God's children. In Jesus' name, amen.

*Therefore encourage one another and build
each other up, just as in fact you are doing.*
—1 THESSALONIANS 5:11

What are a few things you do to build up others? What are things others do that help to build you up?

Teens' natural idealism often leads them to be the first to volunteer their help in crisis situations such as natural disasters. As adults, we can learn much from their example.

• • • • • • • • • •

*"One of the things I keep learning is that the secret of being
happy is doing things for other people."*
—DICK GREGORY, FROM *PATCHES OF GODLIGHT*

PRAYER: Lord, let ____ help others feel the peace and security of knowing that they are accepted by You. In Jesus' name, amen.

DAY 7

Show proper respect to everyone: Love the brotherhood of believers, fear God, honor the king.
—I PETER 2:17

Is this verse saying that you have to respect everyone? What is "proper" respect?

If teens feel respected, they are more likely to treat others with respect. Treating our teens the same way we want them to treat us is the best way to teach them the right attitudes and behaviors. It's important to remember that a person can be respected even though his or her actions may not be.

· · · · · · · · · · ·

"You don't get respect because you want it; you get respect because you earn it."
—MARION ASHES, FROM *MEDITATIONS FOR PARENTS WHO DO TOO MUCH*

PRAYER: Lord, help ____ to respect (himself/herself) and to treat others as (he/she) wants to be treated. In Jesus' name, amen.

Week 47
PRAY

DAY 1

In my distress I called to the LORD; I called out to my God. From his temple he heard my voice; my cry came to his ears.
—2 SAMUEL 22:7

This sounds like a prayer of desperation. When do you do your best praying?

It may take a difficult situation to make a teen turn to God. But the Lord wants us to go to Him to rejoice and thank Him for our blessings as well as turning to Him during times of crisis. Remind your teen that God is available to us both in joy and in sorrow, in success and in failure.

• • • • • • • • • • •

"Prayer is a strong wall and fortress of the church; it is a goodly Christian weapon."
—MARTIN LUTHER, FROM *HEROES OF THE FAITH*

PRAYER: Lord, let ___ know that You are always there for (him/her) no matter what the need. Let (him/her) know that You will listen and show mercy. In Jesus' name, amen.

Answer me when I come to you, O my righteous God. Give me relief from my distress; be merciful to me and hear my prayer.
—PSALM 4:1

Do you ever pray to God without asking for something? What do you pray about then?

If teens can learn to pray always and not just when in distress, they will know Him and themselves better. To have that relationship with God during the good times will prepare them for the difficult ones. Just praising God draws us closer to Him.

• • • • • • • • • • •

"The less I pray, the harder it gets; the more I pray, the better it goes."
—MARTIN LUTHER, FROM *HEROES OF THE FAITH*

PRAYER: Lord, comfort ___ when (he/she) calls out to You. Let (him/her) know that You are there and will answer (him/her).
In Jesus' name, amen.

And the prayer offered in faith will make the sick person well; the LORD will raise him up. If he has sinned, he will be forgiven.
—JAMES 5:15

You have probably prayed for someone to get well and they didn't. What does this verse mean in those circumstances?

God's "big picture" doesn't always include the fulfillment of our short-sighted wishes. It is hard for teens to understand God's will, to see the reason for hardships and pain. But it's in times of crisis that we learn to trust Him. Knowing that God loves them unconditionally will help our teens to trust that God has a plan even when they can't understand it.

• • • • • • • • • • •

*"Prayer is the contemplation of the facts of life
from the highest point of view."*
—RALPH W. EMERSON, FROM *PATCHES OF GODLIGHT*

PRAYER: Lord, hear ___'s prayer, but also let
(him/her) understand that Your will is the best
for us even when we don't understand why.
In Jesus' name, amen.

DAY
4

*Therefore confess your sins to each other
and pray for each other so that you may
be healed. The prayer of a righteous man
is powerful and effective.*
—JAMES 5:16

**Do you confess your sins to friends and family, or only to
God? What difference do you think it would make if we confessed our sins to others?**

Sometimes being accountable to a friend is more real than
confessing to God. Asking others to pray for and with them
is a good habit for teens to develop. They may be more open to
sharing their needs when going through difficult times, and
when their prayers are answered, they will have opportunity to
praise God before others.

• • • • • • • • • • •

*"I have found the greatest power in the world
in the power of prayer."*
—CECIL B. DEMILLE, *MEDITATIONS FOR PARENTS WHO DO TOO MUCH*

PRAYER: Lord, let ___ see the importance
of confessing to You. Let (him/her) also be willing
to be held accountable by others here on earth.
In Jesus' name, amen.

*So I say to you: Ask and it will be given to you;
seek and you will find; knock and the door
will be opened to you.*
—LUKE 11:9

**If this verse is true, why aren't prayers for winning the lottery
or a new car answered?**

Teens may have a difficult time discerning what to pray for. By
striving to know God and His will for them, they will learn to
pray for those things that will benefit them and glorify Him.

• • • • • • • • • • •

"Prayer the key of the day and the lock of the night."
—THOMAS FULLER, FROM *PATCHES OF GODLIGHT*

PRAYER: Lord, help ___ to keep in perspective what
Your will is for (him/her) and to hope for those
things that please you. In Jesus' name, amen.

*In the same way, the Spirit helps us in our weakness.
We do not know what we ought to pray for, but the
Spirit himself intercedes for us with groans
that words cannot express.*
—ROMANS 8:26

**Does this verse help to answer the question from yesterday's
devotion? When you pray, do you allow the Spirit to guide
you?**

Knowing they have the Holy Spirit to guide their prayers is a
huge encouragement for teens to seek God. When they pray
in the power of the Spirit, they will see miracles happen.

• • • • • • • • • • •

*"Prayer must carry on our work as well as preaching:
he preacheth not heartily to his people, that prayeth
not earnestly for them."*
—RICHARD BAXTER, FROM *THE REFORMED PASTOR*

PRAYER: Lord, remind ___ continually that
(he/she) has the Holy Spirit to guide (his/her)
prayers and that You will answer as (he/she)
prays according to Your will.
In Jesus' name, amen.

Do not be anxious about anything,
but in everything, by prayer and petition,
with thanksgiving, present your requests to God.
—PHILIPPIANS 4:6

What are you anxious about? Pray about it right now and present it to God. Is it in God's hands, or do you still have it? You can tell by how anxious you are now.

It's important to know that we are anxious only when we haven't gone to God with our concerns. Learning to trust God to take care of them is difficult for teens, but if they remember to pray as soon as they begin to feel anxious, they will find that their fears lessen and their confidence grows.

• • • • • • • • • •

"Prayer moves the hand that moves the world."
—JOHN AIKMAN WALLACE, FROM *WORLD INVISIBLE*

PRAYER: Lord, show ___ what relief You bring in
times of need. Help (him/her) to always turn to you
right away when (he/she) is anxious.
In Jesus' name, amen.

Week 48
HEART

DAY 1

I will praise you, O LORD, with all my heart;
I will tell of all your wonders.
—PSALM 9:1

You've heard people say that they love something "with all their heart." What do you love with all your heart?

Priorities for teens can be confused and need thought and prayer. We say we love everything from tacos to God, not differentiating the difference in these kinds of affection. Encourage your teen to define what is truly important.

• • • • • • • • • • •

"A grateful heart is not only the greatest virtue,
but the parent of all other virtues."
—CICERO, FROM *PATCHES OF GODLIGHT*

PRAYER: Lord, let ____ dig deep into the depths of (his/her) heart and find what is real and honest there. In Jesus' name, amen.

DAY
2

Test me, O LORD, and try me,
examine my heart and my mind.
—PSALM 26:2

Do you test yourself and examine your own behavior and motives? If you asked God to test you, would His conclusions be different from yours?

It's difficult for a teen to know his or her own heart when moods, preferences, and friends are forever changing. But if they allow God to test them, and then seek His will for their lives, they will make good choices.

• • • • • • • • • •

"The worship most acceptable to God is that
which comes from cheerful hearts."
—PLUTARCH, FROM *THE QUOTATIONS PAGE*

PRAYER: Lord, help ___ to seek Your testing. Let (him/her) allow You to shape and mold (him/her) into what You want (him/her) to be.
In Jesus' name, amen.

DAY
3

My heart says of you, "Seek his face!"
Your face, LORD, I will seek.
—PSALM 27:8

How do you seek the face of a friend? How do you go about seeking God's face?

When friends are face to face, they discern much through each other's countenance that remains unspoken. Teens can learn to know God only by continually seeking His face. For them to desire to know God as deeply as they know a close friend is a good start.

• • • • • • • • • •

I, who live by words, am wordless when
I try my words in prayer. All language turns

To silence. Prayer will take my words and then
Reveal their emptiness. The stilled voice learns
To hold its peace, to listen with the heart
To silence that is joy, is adoration.
The self is shattered, all words torn apart.
—MADELINE L'ENGLE, FROM *WILD FAITH*

PRAYER: Lord, teach ___ to long for You,
to know You and be with You face to face.
In Jesus' name, amen.

DAY
4

Wait for the LORD; be strong and
take heart and wait for the Lord.
—PSALM 27:14

If you aren't waiting for the Lord, what are you doing instead?
Going without God? How do you know when it is time to stop
waiting?

It is hard for a teen to wait for anything, especially God's still, small voice. The clamor of our world so easily drowns God out. We need to remind our teens that when we pray it's necessary to still our minds and open the channel so we can hear God's answer.

• • • • • • • • • • •

"Steady of heart, and stout of hand."
—SIR WALTER SCOTT, FROM *SCOTT-MINSTRE CATHEDRAL*

PRAYER: Lord, give ___ patience to wait upon You
so (he/she) can hear Your answer.
In Jesus' name, amen.

Create in me a pure heart, O God,
and renew a steadfast spirit within me.
—PSALM 51:10

Once we become children of God, all He sees is a pure heart in us. Why, then, do we need to ask for a pure heart and a renewed spirit?

Teens need to know they can ask for God's purification daily because none of us goes through a day without sinning.

• • • • • • • • • • •

"There is a God-shaped vacuum in the heart of every man
which cannot be filled by any created thing, but only by God,
the Creator, made through Jesus."
—BLAISE PASCAL, FROM *365 DAY BRIGHTENERS TO WARM YOUR HOME*

PRAYER: Lord, let ___ see the imperfections in
(his/her) heart and desire to be pure.
In Jesus' name, amen.

Above all else, guard your heart,
for it is the wellspring of life.
—PROVERBS 4:23

How do you guard your heart? How is your heart the well-spring of life?

Many teens live by feelings, not facts. A teen endures a whirl-wind of good and bad emotions every day. Learning how to protect one's heart without becoming bitter is important.

• • • • • • • • • • •

"There are some things that can be learned by the head,
but Christ crucified can only be learned by the heart."
—CHARLES H. SPURGEON, FROM *HEROES OF THE FAITH*

PRAYER: Lord, protect ___ from a broken heart and
mend any damage done along the journey.
In Jesus' name, amen.

DAY
7

*May he strengthen your hearts so that you
will be blameless and holy in the presence
of our God and Father when our LORD Jesus
comes with all his holy ones.*
—1 THESSALONIANS 3:13

**This verse implies that we will feel both blameless and holy in
God's presence. How can knowing this help you in times of
heartache when your spirit is crushed?**

It's easy for teens' spirits to be crushed in today's culture. Only
God can strengthen their hearts to stand firm and resist the
pressure to conform to the expectations of this world. As parents, the most powerful thing we can do is to pray that God will
guard their hearts and minds so they will be blameless and holy
when they come into His presence.

• • • • • • • • • •

*"Never say that you have no time. On the whole it is those who
are busiest who can make time for yet more, and those who love
more leisure time who refused to do something when asked.
What we lack is not time, but heart."*
—HENRI BOULARD, FROM PATCHES OF GODLIGHT

PRAYER: Lord, strengthen ___'s heart so that (he/she)
will stand blameless and holy before You.
In Jesus' name, amen.

Week 49
LOVE

DAY 1

Love the LORD your God with all your heart and with all your soul and with all your strength.
—DEUTERONOMY 6:5

Is it easier for you to love another human being than it is to love God this way? Why is that true for most of us?

Teens form cliques to keep others out. Help your teen to be an example of acceptance. Remind him or her how it feels to be the one excluded and to make every effort not to do the same. We can't truly love God without loving others too.

• • • • • • • • • • •

"Nothing worth doing is completed in our lifetime; therefore we must be saved by hope. Nothing true or beautiful makes complete sense in any immediate context of history; therefore we must be saved by faith. Nothing we do, however virtuous, can be accomplished alone; therefore we are saved by love."
—REINHOLD NIEBUHR, FROM *PATCHES OF GODLIGHT*

PRAYER: Lord, teach ____ to truly love and know You. Help (him/her) to love others as (he/she) loves You. In Jesus' name, amen.

| DAY 2 | *"Because he loves me," says the LORD, "I will rescue him; I will protect him, for he acknowledges my name."*
—PSALM 91:14 |

It doesn't make sense that our loving God would not rescue someone who loves Him. How important is this reason in your list of reasons why you love God?

How consoling it is for teens to know that God is always there to rescue them when they call on Him. If only we would take this to heart when we feel too ashamed to come before the Lord and let Him lift our burdens.

• • • • • • • • • •

"Love is a fabric that never fades, no matter how often it is washed in the waters of adversity and grief."
—EDWIN MARKHAM, FROM *PATCHES OF GODLIGHT*

PRAYER: Lord, give ____ the confidence to call upon You when blinded by the things of this world. Provide a refuge in Your arms and calmness in Your presence. In Jesus' name, amen.

| DAY 3 | *And hope does not disappoint us, because God has poured out his love into our hearts by the Holy Spirit, whom he has given us.*
—ROMANS 5:5 |

When you try to love someone who isn't loveable, how might the phrase, "God has poured out his love into our hearts," help you?

Remind your teen that God has given us the great gift of the Holy Spirit. Help him or her to learn to lean on that connection with the Spirit as a guide through life.

• • • • • • • • • •

"Love is not only something you feel. It's something you do."
—DAVID WILKERSON, FROM *PATCHES OF GODLIGHT*

PRAYER: Lord, help ___ to remember the good works
You have started in (him/her) and to stand against
all evil that might get in the way.
In Jesus' name, amen.

*And we know that in all things God works
for the good of those who love him, who have
been called according to his purpose.*
—ROMANS 8:28

**Many people have trouble believing that anything good can
come out of the bad things that happen to them. How would
you comfort them with this verse?**

Helping teens to see how things turn out in ways they never
imagined will give them hope for the future. Their life's journey may be tough at times, but if they can see the good that
comes as a result of their trials, they'll be encouraged to trust
God whenever they face challenges.

• • • • • • • • • • •

"Love is seeking to make another happy."
—ANONYMOUS

PRAYER: Lord, give _____ the confidence that
You can change everything. Help (him/her)
to rest in that assurance always.
In Jesus' name, amen.

*And I pray that you, being rooted and established
in love, may have power, together with all
the saints, to grasp how wide and long
and high and deep is the love of Christ.*
—EPHESIANS 3:17B

How would you explain to someone how wide and long and high and deep the love of Christ is? Can you think of other words that might help explain how much Christ loves us?

Give your teen an example of the Grand Canyon, a tsunami, or other huge natural wonder or disaster to show God's strength and help him or her understand how powerful He is.

• • • • • • • • • •

"To love someone is to seek his or her highest good."
—LYNDON B. JOHNSON, FROM *GREAT QUOTES FROM GREAT LEADERS*

PRAYER: Lord, help ___ to understand that Your love overflows for (him/her) and that (his/her) relationship with You supersedes all others. In Jesus' name, amen.

DAY
6

Though you have not seen him, you love him; and even though you do not see him now, you believe in him and are filled with an inexpressible and glorious joy.
—1 PETER 1:8

Have you ever really looked forward to seeing someone for the first time because of things you've heard about that person? What else would make you anxious to see him or her? What is it about Jesus that makes you look forward to seeing Him?

Teens, being grounded in the things they can perceive with their physical senses, may not "see" the spiritual as clearly as a mature believer does. As they learn to walk with Him day by day, they will grow into the spiritual awareness that fills us with an inexpressible and glorious joy.

• • • • • • • • • •

"Love is the basic need of human nature, for without it, life is disrupted emotionally, mentally, spiritually and physically."
—KARL MENNINGER, FROM *PATCHES OF GODLIGHT*

> PRAYER: Lord, cause ____ to long for You,
> the One (he/she) looks to for truth, guidance,
> and unconditional love. In Jesus' name, amen.

DAY 7	*Do everything in love.* —1 CORINTHIANS 16:14

What does it really mean to do everything in love?

Jesus gave us the clearest example of love in action in His life and death on the cross. Motivation is crucial in everything we do, and when teens struggle with this issue, point them to the Gospels and to 1 Corinthians 13. If they take these scriptures to heart, what a difference it will make in their lives.

• • • • • • • • • •

'Tis better to have loved and lost
Than never to have loved at all.
—ALFRED, LORD TENNYSON, FROM "IN MEMORIAM"

> PRAYER: Lord, give ____ a heart that overflows
> to others, a heart that is willing to give
> of self and possessions.
> In Jesus' name, amen.

Week 50
PASSION

*Do not withhold good from those who deserve it,
when it is in your power to act.*
—Proverbs 3:27

**Do you consider yourself a generous person? Who are you
most generous with?**

Exposing teens to a variety of charities will give them owner-
ship as they choose whom to help. It's ideal to teach your
children at a young age to give back, but it's never too late to
begin and for parents to be an example when able.

• • • • • • • • • • •

"Hatred and anger are powerless when met with kindness."
—Anonymous

PRAYER: Lord, help ___ to see that giving to others
out of love is actually giving back to You.
In Jesus' name, amen.

*And they did not do as we expected, but they
gave themselves first to the Lord and then
to us in keeping with God's will.*
—2 Corinthians 8:5

What do you think about giving to the Lord before giving to others? Can you think of how giving to the Lord could be doing both?

Being equally generous with money and time is rewarding when it comes from the heart, but to give of yourself results in the richest blessings. Teach your teen to do both.

• • • • • • • • • • •

Let me be a little kinder,
Let me be a little blinder
To the faults of those about me.
—EDGAR A. GUEST, FROM *365 DAY BRIGHTENERS TO WARM YOUR HOME*

> PRAYER: Lord, guide ___ give as pleases You
> and to be faithful in the ministries You put
> on (his/her) heart. In Jesus' name, amen.

DAY
3

But just as you excel in everything—in faith,
in speech, in knowledge, in complete earnestness
and in your love for us—see that you also excel
in this grace of giving.
—2 CORINTHIANS 8:7

Is giving easy for you? What is the easiest thing for you to give? The hardest?

We are naturally self-centered and have to be taught to be generous. For a teen to learn to volunteer from the heart is ideal, but may not come naturally. Find out what your teen is passionate about, and then offer opportunities for involvement in related ministries so he or she feels in control of the decision.

• • • • • • • • • • •

"A kind heart is a fountain of gladness,
making everything in its vicinity freshen into smiles."
—WASHINGTON IRVING, FROM *QUOTATIONS GARDEN*

Prayer: Lord, motivate ___ to excel in everything,
including in the grace of giving.
In Jesus' name, amen.

DAY

4

Remember this: Whoever sows sparingly will also reap sparingly, and whoever sows generously will also reap generously. Each man should give what he has decided in his heart to give, not reluctantly or under compulsion, for God loves a cheerful giver.
—2 CORINTHIANS 9:6-7

Pick a word that fits the way you feel when you give: happy, reluctant, angry, generous, fortunate, etc. Do you always feel the same way when you give?

Do you feel more cheerful when you give generously than when you give sparingly, or vice versa? God promises that when we give generously, we will also receive generously, but that is not to be the motivation for us to give. Let your teen see that you are a cheerful giver who gives from the heart.

• • • • • • • • • • •

*'Twas a thief said the last kind word to Christ;
Christ took the kindness and forgave the theft.*
—ROBERT BROWNING, FROM "THE RING AND THE BOOK"

PRAYER: Lord, help ___ to be a good steward of all
that is given and to be a cheerful giver to those
less fortunate. In Jesus' name, amen.

DAY

5

This service that you perform is not only supplying the needs of God's people but is also overflowing in many expressions of thanks to God.
—2 CORINTHIANS 9:12

When you give, do you usually feel better about what you are doing, or more thankful to God that you can do it?

Teens need to learn that they honor God in their giving and cause others to thank Him. Remind your teen that the Lord sees his or her good deeds and rejoices in the love they express.

• • • • • • • • • • •

"Kindness has converted more sinners than zeal, eloquence, or learning."
—FREDRICK W. FABER, FROM *WISDOM QUOTES*

PRAYER: Lord, remind ___ that all (he/she) has belongs to You and to be thankful.
In Jesus' name, amen.

DAY
6

I know what it is to be in need, and I know what it is to have plenty. I have learned the secret of being content in any and every situation, whether well fed or hungry, whether living in plenty or in want. I can do everything through him who gives me strength.
—PHILIPPIANS 4:12-13

In light of this verse, are you content? Why or why not? Do you believe the people you know best are content?

Talk to your teen about what's happening in our culture, what seems to make people happy and what brings true joy. Make him or her aware of the needs of others so he or she will not only want to help them but also will appreciate what he or she has.

• • • • • • • • • • •

"Be kind to unkind people; they need it the most."
—ANONYMOUS

PRAYER: Lord, help ____ to plan for the future and not to waste what You have given to (him/her). Let (him/her) be content with what (he/she) has and not always want more. In Jesus' name, amen.

DAY
7

And do not forget to do good and to share
with others, for with such sacrifices God is pleased.
—HEBREWS 13:16

What do you think is the difference between giving because God has blessed you with much and giving by sharing something you need yourself? Have you done both?

It can be hard to give, no matter how much you have. Often those who have the least give the most. But if we don't give out of love and with a joyful heart, it doesn't matter how much we have or give.

• • • • • • • • • • •

"Life is short and we have never too much time for gladdening
the hearts of those who are travelling the dark journey with us.
Oh be swift to love, make haste to be kind."
—HENRI FREDERIC AMIEL, FROM *PATCHES OF GODLIGHT*

PRAYER: Lord, show ____ a balance between spending, saving, and giving. Let (him/her) take joy in giving from (his/her) own supply and be wise with (his/her) spending. In Jesus' name, amen.

Week 51
SIN

 Jesus called the crowd to him and said, "Listen and understand. What goes into a man's mouth does not make him 'unclean,' but what comes out of his mouth, that is what makes him 'unclean.'"
—MATTHEW 15:10-11

What would you say is the difference between what the Pharisees understood as unclean and what Jesus said was unclean? What do you think makes a person unclean today?

Learning to curb a sharp tongue will help to keep the heart clean. Words come from the mind, so start there. What do they watch, listen to, and read that might create a behavioral change? Our teens are exposed to things in society today that can turn a heart to stone.

• • • • • • • • • •

"If you tell the truth you don't have to remember anything."
—MARK TWAIN, FROM *WISE WORDS AND QUOTES*

PRAYER: Lord, help ___ to speak with a clean tongue, without ridicule or slander. Let (him/her) speak words of comfort and kindness as Christ showed us to do. In Jesus' name, amen.

DAY

2

Leave them; they are blind guides. If a blind man leads a blind man, both will fall into a pit.
—MATTHEW 15:14

Have you ever been led into sin by someone who didn't think it was sinful? Have you ever led someone into sin because you didn't know any better? How did it work out?

Teens need to know how seductive the devil is, that he doesn't warn them of the lies of the flesh he tells and the misery he will cause. Because sin is often very desirable, it is easy to believe it is also good.

• • • • • • • • • •

"Sometimes you find you're up against it because you back up instead of going ahead."
—ANONYMOUS

PRAYER: Lord, let ___ separate from those who are futile in mind with a darkened understanding and blind hearts. Let (him/her) lead and be led by Your people and witness to those who do not know You. In Jesus' name, amen.

DAY

3

But where sin increased, grace increased all the more, so that, just as sin reigned in death, so also grace might reign through righteousness to bring eternal life through Jesus Christ our LORD.
—ROMANS 5:20-21

Why did grace increase?

The more we sin, the more we need grace because we can't stop sinning on our own. Only through Christ can we have assurance that our teens are saved. When their actions speak otherwise, we trust that God watches over them, and that gives us peace of mind always.

• • • • • • • • • •

Always hold your head up but keep
your nose at a friendly level."
—ERNST LEGOUVE, FROM *WISE WORDS AND QUOTES*

PRAYER: Lord, let ___ not be selfish and begin
demanding (his/her) own way. Let (him/her) be an
example of the grace You have shown (him/her).
In Jesus' name, amen.

DAY 4

But encourage one another daily, as long
as it is called Today, so that none of you
may be hardened by sin's deceitfulness.
—HEBREWS 3:13

Do you think more encouragement would make it easier to be good? Do you know someone who needs encouragement that you can give? How do you feel about giving it?

Sometimes teens think they will feel better if they leave others out. Help teens learn to lift one another up and refrain from bringing one another down. It's so easy to criticize and make fun of one another. But when they find that friend who builds them up, they know and appreciate the difference.

• • • • • • • • • •

The gem cannot be polished without friction
nor the child of God cleansed without adversity."
—ANONYMOUS

PRAYER: Lord, let ___ be an encourager who builds
others up. Don't let the Evil One nullify (his/her)
good works. In Jesus' name, amen.

See to it that no one misses the grace of God and that no bitter root grows up to cause trouble and defile many.
—HEBREWS 12:15

Do you ever feel that you are responsible to keep others from causing trouble? When has someone helped you stay out of trouble?

Being concerned only with our own righteousness actually blocks spiritual growth. Helping someone else to find grace leads us closer to God and to righteousness. Teens need to learn in which areas they are most vulnerable to temptation, and then to avoid those situations. Working with our teens in a sensitive way to identify his or her personal issues and find God's grace will help to keep any bitter root from growing up between us.

• • • • • • • • • • •

"Anger is momentary madness, so control your passion or it will control you."
—HORACE, FROM THINKEXIST QUOTES

PRAYER: Lord, guide ___ to walk away from what is unclean. Create a desire for holiness in (him/her), and keep bitterness from growing between us.
In Jesus' name, amen.

But each one is tempted when, by his own evil desire, he is dragged away and enticed.
—JAMES 1:14

Can we be tempted by something we don't desire? Could the problem lie within us rather than in whatever tempts us?

What we are most drawn to tells us much about ourselves, both positive and negative. Help your teen to recognize his or her strengths and weaknesses related to desires.

• • • • • • • • • •

*"There is a time when we must firmly choose the course
which we will follow or the endless drift of events
will make the decision for us."*
—HERBERT V. PROCHNOW, FROM *PATCHES OF GODLIGHT*

PRAYER: Lord, let ___ submit (his/her) desires to God
so they will not drag (him/her) into the muck and
mire. Keep (him/her) on the straight and narrow
path, no matter how strong temptation may be.
In Jesus' name, amen.

DAY 7	*What causes fights and quarrels among you? Don't they come from our desires that battle within you?* —JAMES 4:1

**According to James, it isn't really the outside things that cause
battles between us and others. It is our own inner desire to have
something that someone else has. What do you think about this?**

Knowing how to battle our own personal evil is true strength.
Preparing teens for the likelihood that they will face this
battle more frequently the closer they become to God will equip
them to resist when temptations come. Help your teen to think
about their own motives when there is dissention.

• • • • • • • • • •

*"Somewhere along the line of development we discover
what we really are, and then we make our decision
for which we are responsible. Make that decision primarily
for yourself because you can never really live
anyone else's life, not even your own child's."*
—ELEANOR ROOSEVELT, FROM *GREAT QUOTES FROM GREAT LEADERS*

PRAYER: Lord, put a new spirit in ___. Let (him/her)
build up instead of tearing down.
In Jesus' name, amen.

$$Week\ 52$$
POWER

DAY

1

"Your right hand, O LORD, was majestic in power. Your right hand, O LORD, shattered the enemy."
—EXODUS 15:6

In what ways can you imagine God's right hand shattering the enemy today? Are you ever the "enemy"? Who is?

Teach teens to recognize when evil is taking control. Looking for the signs and becoming familiar with the enemy's tricks will help them to know when to call on God so they don't fall prey to Satan's ploys.

• • • • • • • • • • •

"There is no power on earth that can neutralize the influence of a high, simple, and useful life."
—BOOKER T. WASHINGTON, FROM *FINEST QUOTES*

PRAYER: Lord, do not let ____ be fearful, but make (him/her) strong and courageous. Give (him/her) the assurance that You are with (him/her) and will never forsake or fail (him/her). In Jesus' name, amen.

He performs wonders that cannot be fathomed, miracles that cannot be counted.
—JOB 5:9

When do you feel like saying this? Do you sometimes think God doesn't do enough for you?

When teens feel that God has failed them, verses like this can remind them how much God was in the battle. Often it's only when we look back after time has passed that we can see clearly how He fought for us and carried us through every situation without our even realizing it.

• • • • • • • • • • •

"Power is of two kinds. One is obtained by the fear of punishment and the other by acts of love. Power based on love is a thousand times more effective and permanent than the one derived from fear of punishment."
—MAHATMA GANDHI, FROM *GREAT QUOTES FROM GREAT LEADERS*

PRAYER: Lord, let ___ be encouraged by your wondrous works and miracles. Give (him/her) the faith that miracles still happen and that they may be witness to one. In Jesus' name, amen.

In the beginning you laid the foundations of the earth, and the heavens are the work of your hands.
—PSALM 102:25

Why is knowing that God created all things important?

For teens to personally know their Creator makes God's power available to them. Through the beauty of creation we get an idea of God's splendor and His power to protect and save us. That assurance will help our teens to stand strong when they are pressured by their peers or their own desires to sin.

• • • • • • • • • •

"Knowledge itself is power."
—SIR FRANCIS BACON IN "MEDITATIONS"

PRAYER: Lord, let ___ glorify You as Creator
and Redeemer, knowing that (he/she) is Your
creation, made in Your image, precious
in Your sight. In Jesus' name, amen.

*He gives strength to the weary and increases
the power of the weak. Even youths grow tired
and weary, and young men stumble and fall.*
—ISAIAH 40:29-30

**Do you think this is talking about being dead tired at the end
of a triathlon, or is it about something else?**

Carrying the torch to reach others for Christ is a daunting task. By leaning on the Lord, our teens will learn how to pace themselves for the marathon of life and also prepare themselves for the hurdles along the way.

• • • • • • • • • •

"Character is power."
—BOOKER T. WASHINGTON, FROM *GREAT QUOTES FROM GREAT LEADERS*

PRAYER: Lord, let Your Spirit of love reign in the
words ___ speaks to encourage others. Remind
(him/her) that when (he/she) is weak You
are strong. In Jesus' name, amen.

*The LORD is slow to anger and great in power;
the LORD will not leave the guilty unpunished.
His way is in the whirlwind and the storm,
and clouds are the dust of his feet.*
—NAHUM 1:3

Does this verse frighten you or give you comfort? Why is that?

Prolonged guilt can keep us from God. For a teen to let go of the past and feel forgiven is the first step in growing closer to God. Recognizing our Redeemer's great power and intelligence to create, destroy, and build up again reminds us that God can heal and restore us when we have sinned.

•••••••••••

*"The sole advantage of power is that you
can do more good."*
—Baltasar Gracian, from *Patches of Godlight*

PRAYER: Lord, let ___ know that You are in (his/her)
midst and rest in Your justice. Let (him/her) see
You in the earth's creation and enjoy You
through all (he/she) experiences.
In Jesus' name, amen.

DAY
6

*So he said to me, "This is the word of the Lord
to Zerubbabel, 'Not by might nor by power,
but by my Spirit,' says the Lord Almighty."*
—Zechariah 4:6

The power Zerubbabel was being given could have been in armies or in position, but it wasn't. Where did Zerubbabel get his power? Which kind sounds more powerful to you? Why?

As teens experience the power of the Holy Spirit working in their lives, they learn to depend on God more and more. The kind of power that depends on social or economic status or military might is temporary and can be overcome by those who possess greater resources or position. The power that comes from God is limitless and eternal and cannot be overcome by anything. What a comfort for teens to know that they are on God's side!

•••••••••••

*"Education is the most powerful weapon
which you can use to change the world."*
—Nelson Mandela, from *Great Quotes from Great Leaders*

PRAYER: Lord, help ___ to see that heavenly power is much greater than any earthly power, that Yours is everlasting and what is of the earth is temporary.
In Jesus' name, amen.

DAY
7

Finally, be strong in the LORD and in his mighty power.
—EPHESIANS 6:10

How strong are you without the Lord? Remember a time when you really felt strong because of the Lord's power, not your own.

We can help teens to recognize God's intervention in their lives so they will be aware of His work on their behalf in the future. Teach your teen that the Lord will never leave them. The hope and trust that confidence gives them will carry them through every situation they encounter in life.

• • • • • • • • • •

"Contemplate thy powers, contemplate thy wants and thy connections; so shalt thou discover the duties of life, and be directed in all thy ways."
—AKHENATON, FROM *PATCHES OF GODLIGHT*

PRAYER: Lord, let ___ be led by You and accept Your instruction and counsel, knowing that You will not lead (him/her) astray. Help (him/her) to trust in You and lean on You daily so (he/she) can see Your unfailing strength. In Jesus' name, amen.

Dear parents,

I hope these words helped get you through this past year. If your year was filled with trials, I pray this book led you to God for assurance and that the questions drew in your teen as well. If your year was spent strengthening a bond with your teen, I hope the issues addressed in this book prepared you for some things he or she might be dealing with.

There is much hope on this page and in this book. Hope for the future—your teenager's future. Hope he or she will develop a healthy relationship with you and with the Lord. My prayer is that this book will help parents and teens communicate with God in their midst. When He is among us our words are gentler, and a cord of three strands cannot be broken.

For the grieving parents who are reading these words, know that many of us have had our share of pain over wrong choices our children have made, and we blame ourselves. Yet Adam and Eve lived in a perfect environment with God as their parent, and they still chose to sin. Their son chose to murder his brother. They were the first dysfunctional family. Children make choices and choices have consequences. If we don't enable our children, they may learn from these errors. We can only train them in the way they should go, and then turn them over to God. My teen clung to her faith through a hard time and is now living a fruitful life, so do not let your children steal your peace.

I received a lot of encouragement from parents to write this book. Many of the stories they shared all sounded strangely familiar. These parent-teen situations are timeless, so we should never feel alone. The more we share and unite, the easier this time of transition will be. We survive with faith, hope, and love.

In Him,
Beth